Make It Big Below The Border

Your Guide to Creating a Fortune in US Real Estate

Nurlan Chulakov

Make It Big Below The Border
Your Guide to Creating a Fortune in US Real Estate

www.MakeItBigBelowTheBorder.com

Limits of Liability and Disclaimer of Warranty
This book is designed to provide reliable and competent information regarding the subject matter covered. However, the advice and strategies contained herein may not be suitable for your situation. Laws and practices often vary from state to state and country to country and you should consult with a professional where appropriate. This book is strictly for informational and educational purposes only. The author and publisher shall not be liable for your misuse of the enclosed material.

Warning – Disclaimer
The purpose of this book is to educate and entertain. While the author and publisher have used their best efforts in preparing this book, they do not guarantee that anyone following these techniques, suggestions, tips, ideas, or strategies will become successful. The author and publisher shall have neither liability nor responsibility to anyone with respect to any loss or damage caused, or alleged to be caused, directly or indirectly by the information contained in this book.

Medical Disclaimer
The medical or health information in this book is provided as an information resource only, and is not to be used or relied on for any diagnostic or treatment purposes. This information is not intended to be patient education, does not create any patient-physician relationship, and should not be used as a substitute for professional diagnosis and treatment.

Publisher
10-10-10 Publishing
Markham, ON
Canada

Printed in Canada and the United States of America

Contents

I dedicate this book to my children –
Anuar, Daria, and Askar.
I hope this book will help them to build their
future.

What Canadian investors are saying about "Make It Big Below the Border"

"I know how hard it is to make a real estate book sharp and easy-to-use at the same time. Nurlan has done it. The bottom line is action, and his book does an excellent job motivating future investors to sacrifice their time and money in buying valuable properties. As a Canadian investor, creating my real estate portfolio in Pittsburgh, I completely share his vision and his ideas about investing in U.S. emerging housing markets."

**Marc O. Dagenais,
Real Estate Investor**

"Chulakov's book is a must read for anyone investing or thinking about investing in real estate as it covers everything an investor needs to know about buying and selling investment properties in the United States. The knowledgeable advice set out in this book simplifies the process of building a successful real estate team and choosing the right properties to invest in so as to make well-informed decisions."

**Mathieu Laquerre,
Canadian Real Estate Investor with Mada Partners**

"This resource gives the clear explanation of how creating the substantial value in real estate leads toward the financial freedom. Nurlan perfectly walks the line between investment principles and practical skills, so you will find a lot of interesting here. I'm sure this book will help many Canadian investors to see the American real estate market in a new way."

**Eric Grenier, CPA,
Canadian Investor in Texas real estate**

"Any investor looking to build their teams and to expand in U.S. real estate markets should get to know the investment methodologies of "Make It Big Below the Border." The tools and insights Nurlan shares in his book are the keys to making things happen and getting results. I'm so grateful for this book, and I believe you will be too."

Ousmane Dicko, MBA,
Canadian real estate investor in Pennsylvania

"An excellent book of showing how to build lifelong passive income in real estate. Nurlan describes all critical stages of acquiring, repairing and managing investment properties in a clear and straightforward way. I highly recommend to everyone who planned to start investing shortly."

Mathieu Bourgoin,
Canadian Investor, Senior Partner at U.S. Simple Maths

"This is an honest and openhearted work describing the real-life process of investing in multifamily properties. I know Nurlan as a smart and hardworking person. I also invest in Woodlawn and South Shore neighborhoods of Chicago. I also know that flipping properties in Chicago is not an easy task for novice investors. So, this book will be useful for those who think that their path to financial freedom goes through the real estate."

Darick Ste-Marie,
Canadian Investor

"This book is written for those investors who seek the most efficient way of using financial leverage in real estate. So, your financial strength may be closer than you think."
-
Pietro Savvides,
North American real estate investor

"This book, written in a precise and pragmatic way, helps to separate the wheat from the chaff in such a serious business as investing in real estate. My advice to those who wish to purchase investment properties, get this book and improve your life."

-   **Marlando Bailey,**
                              Canadian real estate investor

Acknowledgements

I'm profoundly grateful to many people who made it possible for *Make It Big Below the Border* to see the light. Their support helped me undertake this fascinating journey in the world of real estate to reach so many people with the ideas and messages contained in this book. I thank my wife, Aizhan, and our three children, Anuar, Daria, and Askar, for their continuous support and love, which are the biggest strengths in my life. Nothing is more important to me.

I owe my whole-hearted gratitude to my parents, Alieva Roza Murzagalievna and Chulakov Shora Amrenovich, for their never-ending love, their sacrifice for my happiness, and their profound positive impact on my life, my education, and my thinking.

I would like to offer my special thanks to Raymond Aaron for the fantastic opportunity to create my own book. Thanks to your 10-10-10 program, my old dream came true!

I received generous support from Cara Witvoet, the Personal Book Architect. Thank you, Cara, for your valuable assistance and consistent support, and for your words of encouragement and your kindness.

I would like to pay my special regards to Martin Buisson, my business partner. Together, we are creating our mutual real estate portfolio in Chicago. Thank you, Martin, for your strong belief that what we are doing would make a difference.

I would like to show my gratitude to Jose A. Zuniga, our general contractor for our Chicago projects. Despite the severe illness of his closest family member, he stays strong and keeps pushing to realise our projects. Thank you, Jose, for your courage and dedication, for your invaluable collaboration, and hard work.

I wish to thank William Lundgren, our attorney at Jay Zabel & Associates, Ltd. in Chicago, who provides me with a lot of valuable legal advice and support.

I am deeply grateful to Victor Menasce, who is the President of the Ottawa Real Estate Investors Organization (OREIO), one of the leading real estate investors, and the author of *Magnetic Capital* and *The Great Canadian Takeover*, for his intellectual influence on my development as a real estate investor.

I would like to thank God for the blessings, clarity, and support I have felt in bringing forth this book.

Foreword

I'm delighted to present to you *Make It Big Below The Border* by Nurlan Chulakov. If you want to master efficient investment techniques that will help you start off as a professional, this is the book for you! Nurlan gives you a clear pathway to wealth, by teaching you how to invest in 2-4 unit properties in emerging markets in the United States.

You may find yourself currently struggling to find houses with investment potential. You may also not know how to find qualified assistance from builders, real estate agents, and property managers, or how to organize construction and manage properties in the best way.

Make It Big Below the Border will provide you with helpful information and proven methods so you can effectively handle all of these obstacles. Furthermore, you will discover how you can dramatically increase the value of your real estate investment, and how to secure the financing to support it.

What distinguishes this book from other real estate books that you may have read, is Nurlan's deep analysis and understanding of the real estate process, which is reinforced by his practical experience.

Make It Big Below The Border deserves to become a bestseller. I highly recommend this book if you want to invest in real estate - it is a rich source of practical advice, and a valuable guide for easy-to-implement investment actions. Read it now, and learn how you can "make it big" in U.S. real estate!

Raymond Aaron
New York Times Bestselling Author

Getting Started

We are currently undergoing tremendous technological transformations in the information realm, robotics, and life expectancy, which, according to many experts, could lead to significant job reductions in the next 15–20 years. For an increasing number of people, the idea based on the acquisition of assets, which could generate sustainable cash flow to provide them with a sufficient income even if they lose their jobs, becomes more relevant for their well-being.

For me, it seems obvious that to design my professional future using the old rules is no longer a good idea. Unfortunately, a good education or stable work is no longer a safe life-jacket from global changes, which can be caused either by possible financial crises or by the development of new technologies. I realized some time ago that the sooner I start buying valuable investment properties and creating my business, the better it will be for my family and me.

So, I decided to write about my experience in this field, my observations, my actions, and my mistakes. After all, I only recently started investing in real estate in the United States. I am not a real estate guru, and I do not have a multi-million dollar portfolio yet. I had some experience investing in Canada, of course. Furthermore, I successfully began purchasing properties together with my partner in Chicago, and we are quite optimistic about the future of our investment program, since we would create a total equity worth one million US dollars over the next 5–6 years.

We chose our strategy first, tested it once, understood that it worked well, and decided to repeat it again and again. Now we are making plans to expand our operations in Pennsylvania. Here I describe my personal experience, the strategy I followed, and the difficulties and challenges I faced, together with my partner. Thus, the primary purpose of this book is to share my practical knowledge with the same novice investors as I was myself several years ago. I think this position will be relevant to my readers, most of whom are interested in creating a fortune in real estate.

Most authors of books on real estate, which in practice have achieved significant success in investing, are already playing the game on an entirely different level with completely different rules and other realities. Maybe they can give you good advice but, in most cases, they don't practice the same strategy and methods you need now, my dear reader.

It's like small enterprises asking top management of big corporations for advice on how to do business; they, in their turn, will teach start-ups how to survive in the economic realities of small and medium-sized businesses. As for me, I keep acquiring houses with my proven technique, which is described in this book.

I continue to sharpen my investor skills with practice. In addition, I plan to expand to other emergent markets around the country where I will start all over again, like many esteemed readers of this book. Therefore, in remembering what challenges I experienced when I began to purchase investment properties, I just want to help you overcome them.

There are a lot of concerns that keep people from investing in real estate—they don't know where to look for information; they have no time to search for it; or they consider that investment is difficult for them because they lack the necessary knowledge and skills. Some believe that investment in real estate involves significant risk and the danger of losing money, while others think that buying investment properties takes time and needs a lot of money, and many have very limited resources.

I hope this book can help to resolve most of these points. You will also discover my clear step-by-step blueprint for how to create a fortune by investing in US real estate. I believe that *Make It Big Below the Border* will ignite you with enthusiasm, strong motivation, and courage to achieve your goals in real estate.

Don't forget that there are also many print-ready, free bonuses waiting for you with supplementary, skillful information. So, have fun with the journey you are about to take to generate wealth by reading this book.

Let's get started!

Overview – How to Make It Big Below the Border

Real estate is a great option to begin building wealth. However, before starting, every new investor should answer two important questions. Firstly, they must know why they have chosen real estate as an object for their investments. They must be sure that their choice has considerable potential for sustainable growth, providing them with high returns, together with the stability and security of their assets. The second question touches on their choice of the right strategy. Investors must follow a pragmatic and proven system, where they take on only reasonable risks and avoid failures. I will help you to answer those questions because I want you starting the thrilling journey in the world of real estate with enthusiasm and without delay.

Why Real Estate is a Sound and Sustainable Investment

Real estate is one of the safest and tangible assets available for anyone who wants their savings to work for them in the best way to earn a considerable profit. You can enjoy living in your newly purchased property with your family; or you may sell it for profit or maybe rent it for passive income. So, real estate allows you to monetize its value in different ways.

Real estate, as a safe asset, cannot be stolen or brought to another place; it is always associated with the land on which it stands. In fact, some portion of real estate investment covers land purchasing. Gradual but steady population growth leads to the situation where the land in some desirable areas becomes a limited resource. Often, investors see the significant potential of the land they bought and increase its value by constructing an additional house on it, or by erecting a new multi-family property in the place of an old, dilapidated single family population area. So, the land itself has a definite value. As a result, most of the financial institutions recognise this value and lend money on mortgages for properties located in decent neighbourhoods. They also know that a progressive increase in market prices brings stability to the investment. In a 10 to 15- year period, properties can be sold for more. Thus, long-term investment in real estate is a perfect strategy to benefit from property appreciations.

If you understand how things work in real estate, you can permanently create good deals by finding other ways to increase the equity. Investors who are skillful at defining the right markets and the right people on their team are able to raise the value of their investment with a minimal reasonable risk. They will do it through renovation, through changing the destination of the property, and through improving their tenant base, meaning they will rent only to the highest quality tenants. Indeed, real estate is a great tool to provide you with a positive rental cash flow. There is always the need for rental properties; much of the population still prefers to rent, especially the new generation. Thus, investors always have the opportunity to rent properties for a high income.

Real estate has enormous potential in financial leverage because banks provide a broad spectrum of financing on it. In addition, many other private investors can invest their money under the good and safe deals. After a certain level of experience, it's possible to minimise your own financial involvement and invest funds from other individuals who trust you.

Furthermore, real estate is one of the few businesses that enjoy preferential taxation. Creating a proper legal structure helps investors to minimise taxes. They can also get tax-free money when refinancing because, technically, it is not a profit but a new loan. Investing this refinanced money again for purchasing new properties lets investors gain momentum. They also profit from deferring capital gain taxes when selling their properties.

Real estate is an easy-to-start vehicle to wealth and prosperity for new investors. It does not need extensive knowledge and experience. Beginners can learn by doing and performing, and from making mistakes and learning from them. However, they should choose the right strategy, and that is the goal of my book: to provide my readers with a proven step-by-step system that brings them toward their success in real estate.

Why Invest in US Real Estate?

Before we go any further, I would like to clarify the reasons why you should consider investing in American real estate. I am Canadian, and it would be logical for me to tell you about my experience of purchasing real estate in Canada. However, from my point of view, investing in the US real estate market is much more affordable and promising than the Canadian real estate market, even with today's unfavourable currency exchange rate.

In most American cities, especially in emerging real estate markets, I can see properties in decent areas for US$100,000, while it is completely impossible to find something similar in the same price range in Canada. The same kind of property in Montreal, a city where prices are significantly lower compared to Toronto and Vancouver, may cost between CAN$350,000–$450,000, depending on the area. Also, there are some US neighbourhoods where you can spot single family homes selling for US$10,000–$15,000, which is not feasible in any market in Canada. (Further in the text, to simplify the narrative, all prices will be quoted in US dollars.)

By investing in the American real estate market, investors get a much better return on their investments from rents, with respect to the property purchase price. In other words, they receive a larger passive income from rentals while purchasing houses for a lower price. Investors also benefit from applying seller financing, which is more common in the US and allows them to purchase properties for even lower prices.

Despite some differences in laws governing investment and taxation issues between the two countries, there are a lot of options for Canadians to profit and expand in US real estate. All you need is to structure things properly, know the basic principles of creating wealth in real estate, and follow this proven step-to-step system. Examples of many successful Canadian investors can prove it.

In addition, Canadian investors can build their real estate portfolio quicker if they do not have to pay capital gains taxes after each transaction. When selling their properties, they can benefit from deferring the capital gain tax and reinvest saved money in buying more houses. This tax regime is known as the 1031 Exchange.

Another factor to be considered for investing in the US real estate market is the similarity of our social and cultural institutions, which greatly simplifies things for Canadians doing business in the US. We should keep in mind the population potential of our southern neighbour, which is about ten times more than in Canada, with good economic fundamentals for its population growth, which can serve as a guarantee for positive long-term appreciation.

Six Key Elements of *Make It Big Below the Border*

Six essential elements comprise the core of my investment technique. Each of them individually represents a large field of practical knowledge and skills. At the same time, they are the integral stages of a unified strategy around which this book is shaped.

PREPARE

Here, you will learn how to find the right neighbourhood for your investment. You will know how and where to gather valuable information about your real estate market. This section is helpful for building a team of knowledgeable professionals around you.

FIND AND EXAMINE

Once you are sure about where the market you want to invest in is, it is time to take your actions. You will need to find properties with investment potential in your area. I will provide you with some useful tips on how to negotiate a better price and make a proper due diligence of selected properties, so you will have no doubts about buying a really good house with no hidden defects or liens on it.

ACQUIRE

This stage covers all necessary work each investor should do after their offer is accepted. It is the moment to make a final assessment and inspection of the purchased house and renegotiate the price. You will also know how to coordinate your closing and prepare for a potential repair phase.

REPAIR

Through renovation, you are increasing the value of your property. Here you learn how to control this process to make it cost and time effective.

RENT AND REFINANCE

Managing your property from another city or state is the art of all successful investors. This section will advise you how to rent your property to high-quality tenants and supervise your property through the best property manager. After a certain period, when your property is stabilised, you can profit from refinancing. This will be the source of funds for your next house purchase.

REINVEST AND REPEAT

In this part, you will learn how to add value to your property. You will find out how to reinvest your money in your new deals. So, you need to repeat the same transaction again and again until you create a huge equity in real estate.

Chapter 1

The Best Way to Invest in 2–4 Unit Properties

"Life isn't about finding yourself. Life is about creating yourself."
– George Bernard Shaw

Make It Big Below the Border Strategy: General Concept and Methods

There are several well-known, fundamental principles that each investor must follow to be successful in real estate. These are: positive cash flow, substantial property appreciation, and the capacity to buy at the lowest price and sell at the highest. The strategy I will introduce in this book meets all these requirements. This also allows an investor with a modest amount of funding to build up significant capital in a reasonable period of four or five years. Investors can benefit enormously from financial leveraging so the initial investments are ultimately reimbursed in a short time and could be reinvested in something else. Furthermore, investors will take advantage of a more favorable tax regime.

This strategy is so effective that it is widely used by many other investors throughout the United States as a starting point to create their real estate empires; it is known as *Fixer-Upper Rental*. In fact, it is a perfect combination of two of the most common investment strategies in the real estate world—*Buy & Hold* and *Fix & Flip*. Following this plan, investors do not flip; they buy properties requiring repair, fix them, hold them, generate cash flow from them, and flip them later when the right time comes.

This strategy is solid, proven, and has been successfully used for a long time. In fact, I didn't invent anything new here; I just adapted it to your needs and made it easy to realize. All that, and my ideas about exit strategies, make this system more advanced and easy to integrate. This can also be operated from a distance, which makes it convenient for US citizens who decide to invest in other locations and foreign investors. It is very convenient for Canadians because of the territorial proximity and similarity to many cultural, legal, and business aspects. For this reason, and because I am Canadian, I name this strategy *Make It Big Below the Border*.

So, what is the essence of this strategy? It's very simple. As a potential investor, you will buy a property in need of repairs at a low price in the right location. Then, you will add value by repairing but without using your own money for renovation. By that, you will totally renovate and end up with an almost new property that is desired by new *high quality* tenants who are long-term, reliable, and hard-working individuals of families who want a better life for their children. I will show you later how to find such tenants. So, you get great tenants after renovations and add value again by improving the tenant base. Then you will select the right property management company so you are able to manage your business from another city, and even from another country. You will exit in five years when your property is still almost new. Furthermore, you will immensely increase your equity during those five years.

I would like to give you a rough idea how it works. Let's imagine you find a two-unit property in a decent location for $100,000. From here on, all amounts are in US dollars. The price is low because this property needs extensive repairs of an additional $70,000, which we assume is your contractor's estimates. After repair, the value of this property may achieve $280,000. Your investment is $170,000 but, if you apply for financing, you can get about 70%, or $120,000, of this amount. So, your initial down-payment is only $50,000 ($170,000 for the purchase price and the repair cost, minus $120,000 for the loan). Repairs take between three and four months, and then you start to look for great tenants. Finding them to fill two freshly renovated units located in a decent area is not a difficult task. Let's assume these two units start earning $1,350 per month each, or $2,700 for both. Not bad at all! About six months later, you can apply for a regular mortgage, and the bank is ready to refinance 80% of the value of your renovated property, i.e. $220,000. After reimbursing your initial loan for $120,000, you remain with a net cash value of $100,000, tax-free. So, after 9–12 months, you will get another $100,000 in addition to your initial $50,000 investment. You double your investment within a year! And, you're able to reinvest this money by acquiring one more property similar to the first one.

Let's see what happens with your cash flow: mortgage payment will be about $1,180 per month, and all other expenses, like property tax, insurance, management fees, etc., may reach $1,200. If your monthly rent is $2,700, your net profit, after deducting all expenses and the mortgage payment, is about $320 per month. So, the final picture is very inspiring! You get $50,000 in net profit and $320/month as cash flow.

At the end of the first year, you can buy one more property like this one. Remember that you got $50,000 as net profit and, if you decide not to reimburse immediately, your initial investment, which you may have borrowed from your family or friends, can be reinvested again in two more properties. By implementing the same transaction, at the end of the second year, you may acquire a total of three, or even four, similar properties. At the end of the third year, it might be five to six more properties in your portfolio, so the number of your newly acquired houses could increase exponentially!

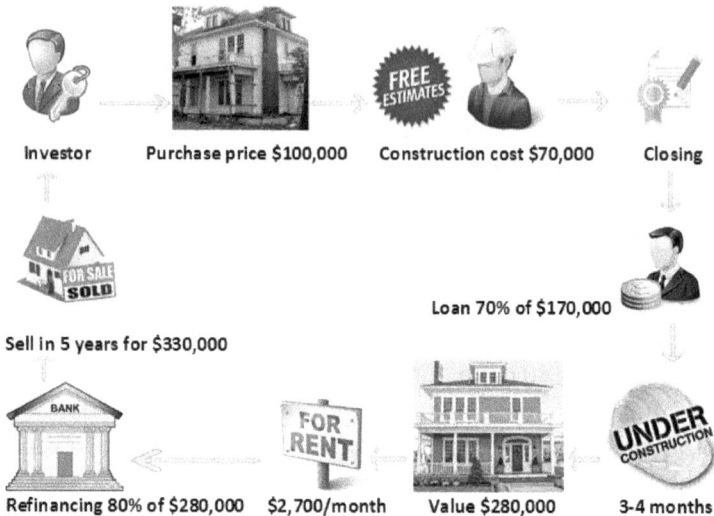

What happens if you decide to sell each property after five years? Each property will be in decent condition. Over time, as you rent the property, the two forces of price appreciation and debt pay down will work together to increase your equity. Coming back to our example with the first house, the balance on a mortgage in 5 years will be about $202,000. However, market value could reach $330,000, if we assume a moderate 3.5% appreciation growth per year. That is $128,000 in equity. After deducting all closing costs from the sale and the commission to your real estate agent, the net profit is about $98,000.

In just one year, your first property will completely reimburse the initial investment of $50,000, as well as bring an additional $50,000 in profit and a $320/month cash flow. After selling it in five years, it will pay an additional $98,000 in net profit. Additionally, the cash flow for five years will be $19,200.

What if you sell ten properties you accumulated during the initial five years of your investment? Selling ten properties after a 5-year period will bring you $980,000 in cash, of which you may reinvest— for example, a 20% down payment on an apartment complex. The selling price of such an apartment complex could be around $4 million, and total rent is more than $20,000 per month. I will develop this idea in my second book, which I am going to dedicate to investing in big apartment complexes.

Main Advantages of This Strategy

This proven system will provide you with the ability to reimburse all initial investment within a reasonable period of nine to twelve months. Just imagine that you start the project, make repairs, settle highest quality tenants, and refinance the property. Here, the magic suddenly works. You immediately return all the money you invested, in just one year, and you make a huge profit. It sounds awesome! We must not forget that this profit is entirely tax free! Because, *technically*, it is not a profit. It is your new liability toward the bank to pay this new regular mortgage and, strictly speaking, it is your tenants who pay that mortgage for you.

You can also scale your business as you may choose to bring other investors or partners in on your next deal. Many real estate investors are happy to be fully reimbursed in one year and still have a significant share in a very secure, profitable asset like your investment property. So, you can increase your financial leverage capacity by attracting other people's money.

The third positive point is the ability to reinvest this money in the next project. With this *revolving scheme,* you don't need to look for money somewhere else to buy your next commercial property. You just reinvest the profit from your previous deal. Then you refinance your second house, and you reinvest again in the third property. You could create your own real estate empire by purchasing several commercial properties each year. This is possible because you can reimburse your money, and because you can attract other investors in your deals. It all depends on your desire and persistence. It works like fuel in a jet engine—and you are creating a jet engine that's going to take off. The more frequently you are able to acquire new properties, the faster your wealth will grow.

My system permits increasing the value of your property through repairs. You will buy it at a low price—at below-market price—and then you will add value through improving the tenant base. Great long-term tenants will make your asset more valuable to future buyers when you decide to sell it. That means you will create significant equity! And that is paramount because great equity gives you leverage for your future deals. Rental income coming from these new projects could serve as a huge real estate wallet for your larger future purchases.

Furthermore, your property provides you with passive income, and that's what a beginner needs to be successful! Each month, starting from the date when you acquire it, your property will provide cash flow because you are going to follow my system. You will rent your house to reliable and responsible tenants. You will control your expenses while managing your property. You will succeed in achieving a positive cash flow. Then, as rent will appreciate over time, the cash flow will grow.

Here, you will learn how to control your expenses efficiently and minimize the maintenance cost. Seasoned investors confirm that maintenance is one of the most troubling issues for beginner landlords. But, in your situation, you have nothing to fear because your property is already renovated; it is almost new.

Make It Big Below the Border allows you to minimize the risk of running out of money during the construction phase. First, you do not invest a big amount of your personal funds. You borrow it from the lender. It could be between 65% and 75% of your purchase price and construction cost. Lenders will ensure that their appraisers approve the scope of work and estimates made by your contractor before financing your project. The appraiser is going to check if the total budget is sufficient to complete construction.

It is a big pitfall for beginner flippers when they finish construction but are unable to sell the property. Their project and money are frozen, and debt service and utility costs demand much more money. However, you will not be stuck with this problem. When you finish construction, you will just rent your property, not sell it. And when you put in great tenants, you just refinance it. That's all.

I'm providing you with the best strategy in real estate to become wealthy. It better prepares you before starting any investment action. You will find the right market. You will create an efficient team. You will set up proper legal structure.

Then, my system helps you to easily find properties, analyze, and close them. It will minimize the risk of the whole operation. Finally, it provides you with a good exit strategy, so you are able to accumulate necessary funds in order to reinvest in larger multi-family and commercial properties.

How Following *Make It Big Below the Border* Can Change Your Life

We will begin by discussing how you can dramatically change your life by investing in the right property. You just need to follow these proven strategies. *Make It Big Below the Border* fully complies with these requirements and your expectations.

Your life will immediately feel more meaningful and fulfilling once you realize that you have created your own successful business. You can continue to work on your favorite job, to make a career, and also build your business in real estate, which could, over time, become a major base for your future businesses.

You will be inspired as well by the idea that you are the owner of beneficial investment properties. As you gain momentum and experience, your real estate empire will expand. Five years later, you will be able to easily buy a multi-million dollar apartment complex, commercial buildings, and even tackle the development of large projects. Is that not exciting?

Just imagine that you do not take any action. You move your focus on other things, not wanting to think about real estate. What is going to happen in five or ten years? Nothing. You and I will be just five or ten years older than we are today. But why continue without the huge equity and profit you would be able to generate in five years by following my system?

Real estate is an understandable and tangible asset that you can own. Therefore, financial institutions and lenders are willing to provide loans under its collateral. It creates financial leverage, which in turn accelerates the accumulation of your own capital. According to *Fortune* magazine, over ninety percent of self-made millionaires in America have made their fortunes in real estate. *Make It Big Below the Border,* along with other successful real estate strategies, could help you pay off your debt, huge medical bills, car, and house loans, as well as create a sufficient retirement cushion.

Finally, it brings you financial freedom: freedom to buy what you want; freedom to be engaged in your favorite area; freedom to pursue any field you wish; freedom to spend more time with your loved ones; freedom to live your dream life; freedom to raise the standards of your lifestyle. Always remember that dreams come true.

How to Improve Your Investor Mindset

As a real estate investor, maintaining the right mental state is one of the most important keys to success, especially when facing the inevitable obstacles of running a business. Look at the most successful people in business and real estate. How do they manage to be strong and motivated? Because they have goals. They have a clear vision of where they are going. You have to know where you are going—and then stay the course. Unfortunately, staying motivated can be really hard at times. But remember that success is the only path, and failure is not an option. Don't forget why you started, know where you are going, and stay focused on the prize. Success in real estate takes time, persistence, and mental training. Believe in yourself and remember that you are capable of great things.

Emotional Intelligence

As practice shows, it is not a lack of specialized knowledge and experience, and not a lack of resources, such as money and time, that prevents people from getting rich. The most critical factors are actually their social environment and their emotional state. It is extremely important to know this. Dedicate time to improving your emotional intelligence: the ability to perceive, control, and evaluate your emotions. Pay attention to your feelings and connect them with your thoughts. Listen to your intuition. Practice deciding how to behave. Be open-minded and agreeable. Do not let negative emotions influence your investment decisions. Decrease your level of stress by improving your emotional skills.

Environment

Your social environment is what builds your character and determines how you react to things. If you surround yourself with cool people, you will become cool. That is why there are wealthy neighbourhoods and clubs where only wealthy people go. The rich mainly connect with like-minded people; not because they hate poor people, but because they want to be successful and stay so. We often seek an environment that is psychologically comfortable for us, so try to be more selective about who you spend your time with. The people you choose to surround yourself with will influence your life. Try to contact and create good relationships with other seasoned investors and entrepreneurs who have been in business for more than five years. Today, thanks to the Internet, it is much easier.

Making Lemonade from Lemons

If, however, something goes wrong, do not despair. Just try to make lemonade out of lemons. Think carefully about the good things you have and about the good people surrounding you. Try to visualize how you can reduce the importance of the difficult situation you are in. Try to visualize your goals. It's going to help. Frustration will be replaced by a strong determination to solve your problems in creative and positive ways.

Analysis Paralysis

Remember that you will need to overcome the *paralysis of the analysis* when you start searching for investment properties. Although the numbers might tell you that you have chosen an awesome house, you will probably still doubt that your choice is correct. Analysis paralysis is going to freeze your will and your actions. You could lose a lot of time, miss many good deals, and ruin good rapport with your team members. However, there is only one solution. You must be strong and courageous; do not hesitate to put in the offer. If something is wrong, you will always have an opportunity to pull out of the deal later.

Making Mistakes

Do not be afraid to make mistakes. It is a required element of your development and of your establishment as a successful investor. Read Robert Kiyosaki's book, *Rich Dad's Guide to Investing*. He explains why making mistakes can be useful when you start your new venture. It's one of the reasons why 'A' grade students often end up working for 'C' grade students in real life. I'm joking, of course. But there is some truth in this. So, don't be afraid to make mistakes, to hire the wrong real estate agent, to make an offer on a wrong house, or to choose the wrong materials for repair. You are gaining a positive experience. In any case, you will succeed in real estate. Just keep going. Don't worry. Dare. Be Brave. Everything will be fine.

Why Investing in 2–4 Unit Properties is a Wise Decision for Beginners

When I talk about 2–4 units of real estate, I am referencing the spectrum of properties with two, three, and four units, or apartments, under one roof. They are often called duplexes, triplexes, and quadruplexes. They are multi-family, but not quite commercial properties (at least, from the lenders point of view).

So, why is investing in them the best solution for you? It's very simple. For beginners, who only want to fix and flip, the best solution is single-family homes. There is less risk and less money to spend on rehab. But to receive passive income from rent, to profit from property appreciation, and to build your wealth in equity, the 2–4 unit properties are the best choice. They are the most effective and perfect real estate tool; you just need to follow my system.

Compared with single-family houses, 2–4 unit properties have many advantages. First, they have higher cash flow from rent. A single-family, 4-bedroom house, as a common example, can be rented for $1,400 a month (depending on the area, city, and state). After deducting all expenses (like a mortgage payment, vacancy, all utilities, service, and maintenance costs), in most cases, it becomes negative cash flow. Rather than collecting profit, the investor faces losses each month. You shouldn't forget that one of the criteria in *Make It Big Below the Border* is a substantial positive cash flow. Therefore, the option of single-family homes is not suitable. But a duplex in the same area, with two 3-room apartments, may bring you rent of about $2,600 a month. Your cash flow immediately switches into a positive zone.

Often, rent correlation to purchase price for 2–4 unit buildings is higher than for single-family homes. In this case, it means that you will get more cash flow from rent and put less on the down payment. (Normally the rent to price ratio is used to compare properties of the same kind in different areas and cities. You may need it when selecting cities with affordable purchase prices and the highest rent. However, it is also useful for comparing various types of properties in the same area.)

Besides, investing in 2–4 unit buildings creates economies of scale by consolidating and minimising all possible expenses for renovation and maintenance under the roof of one property. For example, if you have three single-family houses as opposed to one triplex, you have three roofs to be repaired and three lawns to maintain. So, at an economic scale, the triplex is more cost effective. You can also afford to hire management companies to manage your tenants because of the larger cash flow from the 2–4 unit house.

Your risk is also significantly reduced in proportion to the number of apartments under one roof. If you have a single-family house and you lose your tenant, you have lost 100% of your income. From that moment, you are responsible for paying mortgage and utilities. If you have a triplex and lose a tenant, you still have two sources of cash flow to pay your expenses.

Also, in some areas, the requirements for decorative finishes on single-family houses have risen considerably. Customers often require very high-quality design, and sometimes custom finishes. It dramatically increases the repair budget. The situation with duplexes is much easier. You can make a beautiful design renovation in the apartment on the first floor, and a simpler finish on the second floor. Often, you will spend almost the same amount of money on both the renovation of one duplex and one single-family house.

The inventory of 2–4 unit properties on the market is comparable to the inventory of single-family houses. They have almost the same privacy, backyards for children to play, garages, and laundry facilities. Duplexes and triplexes are also desirable, sometimes even more so than single-family houses, because people often want to live closer to their parents, children, relatives, or friends.

Duplexes and triplexes are also easier to sell. It is much more difficult to sell a complex with more than four units. You can only vend them to investors. Nevertheless, there are a lot of individual buyers looking for duplexes and triplexes compared to the relatively smaller number of investors looking for larger buildings. When it comes time to sell, you will want to do it quickly, receive your money, and move on.

Today, with a big supply of available, for-rent dwellings on emerging real estate markets, tenants have a wide choice of single-family, duplexes, and apartment complexes. Of course, they often choose in favour of single family and duplexes. They want privacy and don't want to live under or above other tenants. However, sometimes, depending on the area, duplexes and triplexes are more affordable to them than single-family homes.

A Buyer's Market, a Seller's Market.
When Is It a Right Time to Invest?

The real estate market goes up and down, and sometimes stays flat. Although it's wise to try and predict market behavior for the coming year or five years, we never know for sure where the market will go. But is this an obstacle that prevents you from making a fortune in real estate? Absolutely not. Markets should not dictate how much money investors make. Markets dictate the strategy of how you invest in real estate. If you have a proven system, it provides you with a reliable pathway to be protected against all possible scenarios. It's the kinds of deals you make that are more important. *Make It Big Below the Border* shows you exactly how and when to make good deals.

Like any industry, real estate is cyclical and based on supply and demand: there is a *buyer's market* and a *seller's market*. The buyer's market is split into two phases: Phase 1, when the real estate market is on the up, oversupplied by houses with stagnating or slightly decreasing prices; and Phase 2, when prices are falling rapidly until they hit bottom. Respectively, the seller's market has its own Phase 1, from the bottom of the curve, when the market is starting to recover; and Phase 2, when the market is thoroughly hot and still moving up.

Phase 1
of the Buyer's Market

Phase 2
of the Seller's Market

Phase 2
of the Buyer's Market

Phase 1
of the Seller's Market

OVERSUPPLY – Phase 1 of the Buyer's Market
RECESSION – Phase 2 of the Buyer's Market
RECOVERY – Phase 1 of the Seller's Market
EXPANSION – Phase 2 of the Seller's Market

Though it is hard to predict the future of the market, identifying the correct cycle and phase the market is in at any given moment is still very crucial for each investor. You need to be perfect in choosing the right moment when to enter and when to exit a project.

So, the best time to acquire a property is in Phase 2 of the buyer's market as it is much easier to find motivated sellers then, and it's still possible to buy at a 50%, or even 70%, discount. At Phase 1 of the buyer's market, I do not recommend you buy properties. However, I recommend you to be prepared to buy and to mobilize yourself and your resources because the market will soon enter Phase 2.

If you are in a hot seller's market, it will be more difficult to find motivated sellers. When prices are moving up, sellers prefer to bid on their properties through MLS, which means you are competing with real estate agents for inventory. In this case, you have two options: either to implement more complicated marketing tactics to find good deals, or to find other areas and cities with affordable prices.

If you are in a stagnant, flat market, it is not a bad time to make deals. But you should purchase properties at 70% of their market value. That protects you if the market begins to change.

When it's time to sell your investment property, the only best time is Phase 2 of the seller's market. Then you can get the highest selling price for your house. Never buy a property at the top of the market and sell it after it hits bottom. Independently of the cycles, your property continues to generate cash flow, meaning you are receiving a passive income from your property. This will allow you to stay safe until you reach the desired phase. There is an important rule in real estate: it's quite impossible to sell properties above the market price. Meanwhile, you still can find undervalued properties when you're looking to buy. Investors make money when they buy—not sell—their properties!

Regardless of areas where you want to invest, the general principle is the same: invest in the market at the right cycle, find properties with motivated sellers, buy at a discount, add value through renovation, generate cash flow from rents, and exit later during the right cycle for selling.

Now you know more about my strategy. You learned about real estate cycles and which cycle is more preferable for entering into a deal, and which one is right for your exit strategy. Now, I suppose, you have a concern: where to find such markets. I dedicated the next chapter to answer this very question and to make you comfortable in recognizing and selecting the right markets with high investment potential. I will introduce you to the key principles of how to pick them up so you can do it yourself later. So, welcome to my next chapter.

Chapter 2

How to Find the Right Market

"Don't buy the house; buy the neighborhood."
– Russian Proverb

Finding Right Market Made Easy, General Principles, and On-line Resources

In the previous chapter, you learned about the possibility of applying my investing strategy in only certain cycles of the real estate market. It is much better to buy when the market is at the bottom and to sell when the market is at its top. However, most want to buy close to where they live, regardless of which phase the market is in at the moment. So, what if you reside in an area where the market is not in the most optimal stage? What if your local market has investment properties that will produce only poor returns? On one hand, you may be able to choose the most sophisticated marketing practices to identify distressed properties in hot markets and still turn a profit. Many seasoned investors can utilize direct mail campaigns, driving for dollar, auctions, tax liens, buying from wholesalers, and many other techniques to phenomenal ends. And you can also apply all those methods but all while at the right market cycle. Moreover, only use them when you have enough experience in real estate; these techniques require immense preparational time and specialized knowledge. However, if your goal is to start now, without complicating your way to success in real estate, my advice is to find another area where the market is at the right point in its cycle. Find another area where you do not need to make all this extra effort and incur all these additional expenses just to find great deals.

There is good news: you can find a wonderful market at almost any time; cities and towns around the country are rarely in the same market cycles. Even different areas and suburbs within one city can be in different cycles. There are cities, towns, and suburbs that are booming now, and there are also declining, stagnating, and slowly recovering areas. So, it is possible to find a great market at any time. As I said earlier, the key to making a huge profit is to recognize which phase each market is in. Of the four market phases, you can only make a fortune by buying properties in one: Phase 2 of the buyer's market. Usually, investors call it the *emerging* market. Many investors have invested and enormously profited in emerging markets. Typically, the prices for single-family houses and duplexes in these markets do not exceed $100,000–$120,000. If prices supersede this range, there is often not enough space to create great equity. You should remember that only investing in emerging markets is a desirable but ultimately insufficient condition for the successful real estate investor. You must also understand other important indicators before you begin searching for the right markets.

Make It Big Below the Border offers the most simple and efficient plan for you to find an extremely promising, high-potential market. I have divided it into two sections. The first section delves into the macro-level economic parameters of a given market, such as population growth and density, job growth, and unemployment rates. The second section scrutinizes the housing market of a chosen neighborhood: its vacancy rate, median home prices, home appreciation, crime rate, and availability of good schools. I will explain all these factors in greater detail further on in this chapter, but by the end you will have an efficient, selective pathway to choose a great neighborhood for your investment.

Online Resources

When employing my system, you will need to know where to gather information about your investment sector. The simplest way is to just Google it!

I also recommend using the official sites of the Bureau of Labor Statistics of the US Department of Labor (www.bls.gov), and the US Census Bureau (www.census.gov).

You will also need to ensure there is enough inventory in your market. You can research this information by consulting real estate sites such as Redfin.com, Realtor.com, or Trulia.com. Just select your neighborhood, adjust the filters as necessary, and you can see how many properties are currently available. You can also check price range for all existing properties, as well as the average price for sold properties in the last six months, which is also important.

To verify if a rental property is a good investment and to compare rents at any given location, I would recommend you use Rentometer.com. This is an outstanding online tool investors can turn to for accurate data on how to set their rents. The Rentometer numbers provide median rent and compare with indicative rent markers. It also shows a map of the area and other similar properties' rents in the neighborhood.

If you want to go deep in due diligence of your market, you can elect to locate and download a city's CAFR, or Comprehensive Annual Financial Report, which is a set of US government financial statements that contain the financial report of a city and other public institutions. You can use this information to verify whether the city is economically stable and will support your investment goals and strategies. CAFR provides you with an immense amount of detailed data regarding a city's operations, management, plans for improvement, demographics, and more. You can find a CAFR by googling it with your city's name.

Let's continue our exciting journey to find you a perfect market.

Analyzing Macroeconomic Parameters

Population Growth

According to my system, you should preferably choose a neighborhood that is a part of larger Metropolitan Statistical Areas with populations no less than 300,000 habitants. You should also select an area with a high population density, which will increase demand for local real estate. This will ensure your rental base is a large, diverse population. You may easily Google to find the US metropolitan cities most suited for your investments. Some investors are comfortable with buying real estate in the towns with populations of less than 100,000 but, in my opinion, such areas are attractive for investment only in three cases: first, when the area is a beautiful and adorable place to reside. Second, when the neighborhood is a suburb of a larger city. Third, when you know for sure that big corporations will be moving in, and you can reliably predict the job market will increase in the area.

You can verify trends in population changes in every selected neighborhood using the US Census Bureau website. If the population of a neighborhood is decreasing, not only will you have problems finding renters, it is an indication of economic and social vulnerability in that locale. So, you need to find cities with population growth that exceeds the national average.

It is important to know the reason why there is a population increase in your neighbourhood. If it is simply because birth rates are exceeding death rates, that won't work. New household formation is what is crucial, where the number of people moving into the city is more than the number moving out. This is a good sign that a given neighborhood has something to offer to attract more potential renters. Furthermore, companies looking to open new facilities or new branches often look to areas with high population growth, and this causes an increase in commercial real estate demand as well.

Where to find out: You can find information about population trends on official websites of the US Census Bureau and the Bureau of Labor Statistics.

Your goal: Find your target market in the cities with a population of more than 300,000 and a sustainable population growth.

I recommend you gather all information about transport, education, and sports infrastructures in your chosen market. Is there any large or international airport, or a commercial port in your sector? Has a city projected an expansion program for rail and transit systems? Are there any major league professional teams in hockey, football, basketball, or baseball in the city? Does a city expect major enlargements of university facilities, like the construction of new campuses, soon? Almost all plans for hospitals, schools, shopping, and public infrastructure development will impact property values in an area.

Where to look: Google

Your goal: You should pay attention to any significant extension in sport, education, and transport facilities, and take note of the exact location these developments are proposed for. In future, you will buy your investment properties within a few blocks from those sites.

Job Growth and Unemployment Rates

Job growth is a paramount factor you must consider while selecting your real estate market. Check this information for your area with the official site of the Bureau of Labor Statistics, in the table of employees on nonfarm payrolls by state and metropolitan area.

Through other internet sources, you may find information about the nature and stability of job growth. As the most stable jobs are in the fields of government, education, and healthcare, try to find information about local authorities' plans to develop the infrastructure and to construct new schools and hospitals in your area. If a county intends to build a new hospital, it would be a wise decision to purchase your investment property somewhere nearby as you have a high probability of getting long-term tenants.

The essential point is that the presence in your market should encompass at least six or seven big American or international corporations. It has to be their main product and brand facilities, and expanding to their headquarters, not just their shops, distribution centers, or local branches. You may use various search engines, including Google, for this information. It is also important that the majority of those corporations work in different fields. Not all of them should operate in the same field such as the oil sector or car production. The potential crisis in that industry might cause significant job cuts, so you need to find cities with a diversified economy. I also recommend you figuring out whether big and medium-sized companies are moving into or out of the city, and what the state and local governments are doing to attract new businesses. When one *white collar* professional is employed, three to four *blue collar* service provider jobs are created to support him or her. For example, if two thousand new non-agricultural jobs are set up in your investment area, the total employment increases to eight thousand.

Unemployment is another major indicator of a market's economic health. If people do not have jobs, they cannot pay their rents. The most important task is to figure out the unemployment trend in your area. If it is rising, it can be deduced that a market has become less attractive; on the contrary, decreasing unemployment is a sign of market recovery. It is exigent to compare unemployment rates with the changes in total employment in a given area. Sometimes the unemployment rate could be stable and even decreased, which is a good sign by itself, but the global picture could be frustrating due to a dramatical drop in the number of working people.

Where to Find: You can find the unemployment rate for your city at Bestplaces.net. The best source for tracking job growth trends for the last two years is the official website of the Bureau of Labor Statistics (Table: Civilian labor force and unemployment by state and metropolitan area.).

Analyzing Local Housing Statistics

Understanding the local market statistics is paramount to identifying your target real estate market. It will also help you to have an idea about the direction in which your market is moving.

The first thing you need to start with is to study the market inventory. It is the quantity of houses listed for sale through Multiple Listing Service at any given time. Don't choose a market with low inventory: markets not sufficient for 2–4 unit properties and in your price range. If you ignore this advice, you will be stuck in the coming two or three years while you are investing in your target area. If you face troubles finding your investment properties, you cannot create momentum by making more deals and giving more jobs to your contractor, realtor, or other members of your team. The overflow of available houses for sale provides you with the high speed and long-term duration of your investment program. It is important to keep in mind that every market is local and might be different. As you see inventory levels dropping, consider it an indication that your target neighborhood may be moving towards a seller's market.

When you search markets with high inventory, take a look at the availability of distressed inventory for a price less than $100,000–$120,000. As I mentioned earlier, you should not exceed this price range. If you do, you will not have enough space to profit from significant equity that you are going to create by renovating your property.

At the same time, take a glance at how many properties sold and how many are pending compared to the active listing. Firstly, it helps you get a clear picture of how active your target market is at the moment, and whether it is stagnating or warming up; and secondly, it gives you an idea as to how pushy your negotiation tactics should be when it is time to place your offer. If you encounter a situation where many properties have been sold or are pending, it means the market is pretty active and good deals do not last long. If there is a negligible number of sold houses, compared to the active listing, you should choose a different approach. I will touch upon these alternative approaches in detail in the next chapters.

Another key metric to watch is the average days on the market, which is the number of days for which a property appears on MLS for sale before it stands pending under the contract. Try to select your target area in which most houses have not been on the market for longer than 180 days. Obviously, you could find a property which has been on the market longer than six months, and it is even desirable as you will have more chances to negotiate the best purchase price. But average days on the market for your sector should not exceed this level. If the average level rises to over 12 months, it is a sign of a housing crisis in your neighborhood.

Where to find: Redfin.com; Trulia.com; Zillow.com.

Your goal: Find your target market in an area with high inventory. Simultaneously, take a look at the availability of distressed inventory for the price less than $100,000–$120,000. Find out a number of pending and sold houses for the last three months. Select the area where the average amount of days on the market does not exceed six months.

Gauge Whether the Rent is High Enough

Owning rental property is all about cash flows and your return on investment. High-cost markets are not suitable for investors who wish to rent their properties simply because of their low price to rent ratio. You should avoid situations where you pay a high purchase price compared with low rents. You are not going to cover your expenses, which includes a high mortgage payment, and your property will likely become a liability nightmare for you. That is why I would suggest you opt for emerging, developing markets with relatively low prices, and look carefully at the rents in your sector. They must be high enough so that you can profit off them each month. In the Chicago market, where I am expanding my investment activity now, I selected properties with three bedrooms and areas where the rent is a minimum of $1100–$1200 a month.

Where to find: The best way to determine market rents for your target area, is to look at different internet real estate sites, like Trulia.com, Zillow.com, or Realtor.com to see available rentals. You can find the most accurate information about rents at Rentometer.com. This website is very helpful when you start looking for properties in a selected area because it provides you with rent comparatives.

Your goal: Figure out if rent is high enough for two and three bedroom units in your target area.

Vacancy Rate

A vacancy rate performs as a significant indicator of the health of a real estate market. It is the percentage of all vacant premises in relation to all leased apartments in a rental property calculated within one year. There are three reasons why apartments are idle. First, the local market doesn't allow to find decent tenants, even when units are ready for rent. Second, the problem is in the apartments which need an extensive repair. The third reason is bad management that leads either to the deterioration of the property or to the escaping of good and long-term tenants. Each neighborhood has its own vacancy rate, and that information is available for the public. I suggest you find a neighborhood with a maximum vacancy rate of 10%. If it is higher than 10%, it probably isn't the best market to invest in. Locations with such a high vacancy rate suffer from crime, lack of good schools, and excessive unemployment. In good and decent areas, you could choose a property with a higher vacancy because the rate will fall when the improvements are complete. But you should aim for a lower rate when you are looking at an area. You can also monitor the trends to see whether vacancy rates are increasing or decreasing overall.

Where to find: Vacancy rates in each state and city are available on the website of the U.S. Census Bureau. To figure out a vacancy rate for a particular neighborhood, I recommend you to Google the information.

Your goal: You need to select the area where the vacancy rate is less than 10%.

Median Home Cost and Home Appreciation

Another important metric to track in your local market is the median sale price. It is the price in the midway point of properties sold over the last three months (or another period, if needed) in a specified location (by city, county, or zip code). While you are interested in the properties with the lowest price, you should find areas with the highest median sale price. The lower the median sale price, the less potential equity a given market has because investors cannot count on high selling prices after renovating their properties. And vice versa: markets with higher median sale prices return higher prices for renovated properties. You can find median sale prices through Trulia heat maps. Just Google the name of your city and Heat Map, and then choose Trulia website.

Another important criteria for choosing properties and markets is property appreciation—the increase in the value of your property over time. This growth can occur for a number of reasons, including increased demand, declining supply, or as a result of changes in inflation or interest rates. Logically, you need to find a neighborhood with the highest home appreciation. Your equity will increase enormously. In my opinion, this is a good tactic if you have no plans to buy more properties in future in your market. It is still okay if you are just buying few houses before looking for another area. However, if you want to stay in your neighborhood longer, it might be difficult to find inventory in future, because prices will skyrocket. You need to choose the neighborhood with a moderate and sustainable growth in home appreciation. The most important thing: it should not be negative.

Where to find: You can find the median sale price by Googling the name of your city and Heat Map. For example, Philadelphia Heat Map. Then you choose Trulia website. You can find home appreciation rates for your area through NeighborhoodScout.com, but fees may be applied.

Your goal: To find the market with the highest median home cost and with a positive home appreciation rate.

Crime Rate and Schools

Crime Rate

Another important indicator to keep in mind is the crime rates in your target neighborhood. Buying your investment property in the highest crime area could be risky, and properties there have little value because people do not want to live in such dangerous neighborhoods. Becoming aware of neighborhood crime helps you to avoid costly mistakes in assuming that you can get great and stable tenants later and can attract the necessary loan for a property in an area you think is safe but, in reality, is not. I suggest you pay particular attention to property crimes. Try to avoid areas with high risk for your potential property to be damaged and vandalized. Today, thanks to many online resources, it is easy to find neighborhood crime statistics and even compare neighborhood safety ratings.

Nevertheless, when it is time to buy a property, I recommend asking the opinion of your local team members, especially your property manager and your contractor. Sometimes the crime situation in a given area might change from block to block, such as poor inclusions in a decent area and vice versa. With good knowledge of the neighborhood, your property manager can tell you whether it is safe enough for them to manage your property. Your contractor shares their opinion with you on whether they are comfortable leaving their tools and materials there at night during repair works. Another valuable source of information is your neighbors. Some of them, as occasion offers, are ready to talk your ear off about their neighborhood. Don't be shy about asking if they like living in the area or how safe they think it is.

Where to find: You can locate the crime rate in your target market at CrimeReports.com; NeighborhoodScout.com; SpotCrime.com; and at Trulia Heat Map.

Schools

While you start selecting your target neighborhood, remember one important point. Because you want to have great tenants—the tenants who have children and care about their children's future—it is inescapable that your property should be located in an area with great schools. I consider not only public but charter schools as well. So, try to select an area with a school that has an excellent reputation. When you are looking for properties, it would be a good idea to buy them near those schools because that is where your great tenants would like to live. Furthermore, police cars often patrol near schools, which adds better protection to your property.

Where to find: GreatSchools.org is an outstanding online resource to find the list of all schools in your area and their school rating based on test scores, student academic growth, and college readiness. Trulia.com also provides you with the map of your area with all listed schools, and marks them in different colors according to their ratings.

As investors, we want to know as much as possible about the city's job growth, unemployment, crime, industries, primary source of income, other demographic information, and development plans for the future. In this chapter, I tried to assist you by focusing on crucial issues and packing them in a convenient and easy way. In the beginning, all this may seem daunting and to be a lot of work. However, you need to do some research and dedicate enough time for that. You will be paid amazingly for your efforts. Nevertheless, you do not need to do all the work alone. You will be strong enough and more efficient as a real estate investor when you create a victorious *Star Team* around you. So, in the next chapter, we will talk about how and where to find these incredible people for your team.

Chapter 3

How to Build Your Team and to Make It Operate Effectively

"Talent wins games, but teamwork and intelligence wins championships."
– Michael Jordan

When starting out in real estate investment, it is of paramount importance to have a team of experts and professionals to assist you in achieving your goals. It is your victorious *Star Team*, which consists of a real estate agent, attorney, accountant, lender, general contractor and property manager. All these key professionals will make you more successful and create more wealth if you carefully pre-screen them in advance and select the best ones. Leveraging other people's knowledge, competence, and time is crucial for your development as an investor and for growing your capital, while the wrong choices may cost you money, stress, and time. There are many factors you should pay attention to when creating your team, and we will consider them all diligently in this chapter.

How to Find Your Real Estate Agent

The number one person is your real estate agent. You should create your victorious Star Team starting with them. A good real estate salesperson knows that whatever is good for you will be good for them as well. If you don't succeed in buying your first investment property, they won't be paid either. Your realtor is only compensated when you finally make a transaction. If you are not happy buying the right property, and that house doesn't bring you a profit, you will find another property agent for your next deal or when you need to sell the first property. Every real estate broker knows they should be doing the best job on time for you. There is then a chance you will work together in all your future deals. The increasing trust between you and your agent will save a lot of time for you and helps you to gain momentum in your real estate operations. There are several other reasons why you need this person. First, your agent is an incredible source of contacts. During your first meeting, ask them to refer you a good general contractor, a good attorney, and property manager. Tell them you are new in the city and you need to build the reliable and knowledgeable team to move forward and develop your investment plans. Ask only for those three professionals because they are crucial to start immediately. You will later ask for other experts, like inspectors and insurance brokers, when you come close to acquiring your first house. The second reason is the opportunity to get useful information about local markets. You can find out a lot of facts and statistics online, but I prefer to talk directly with my realtors about the target neighborhood I want to invest in. Often, the agents provided me with useful advice and guided me in right direction. Sometimes I even printed out a detailed map of the area and asked the agent to circle bad and good sectors in each particular neighborhood. In many cities and counties across the country, the real estate market might vary from block to block. So, with the assistance of my agent, I review all interesting areas on the map—street by street and block by block. It helps me to better understand my market. The more knowledgeable information about your target market you have, the more chances you have of avoiding mistakes when buying your property. Even in decent neighbourhoods, it is still possible to find poor spots, and vice versa; inside some crappy sectors, you may find decent blocks. Typically, your broker should know and warn you about such locations. Nevertheless, if I notice that my agent feels lost on the map and cannot define the good and bad blocks, I question their expertise about the neighbourhood.

Furthermore, I ask real estate agents to inform me about the current market trends—whether the market is moving up or down, and how many days or months it usually takes on average to sell a property in a particular area. Also, your real estate agent is a constant source of good deals. They have permanent access to MLS, so you just need to manage your agent right and insist they provide you with timely information about new listings. In emerging markets, it is still possible to get good deals listed on MLS because the competition for good properties is not so intense as in hot markets. I like deals coming from my agent's listings. MLS provides certain transparency, and you can get a lot of useful information about any property even before you put an offer on it. Another significant benefit of a real estate agent is the comparatives. When you put an offer on a property, you should ask your agent to provide you with the Comparative Market Analysis (CMA), which consists of the active listing and the listing of similar properties sold in your area during the last six months. This analysis gives you a realistic picture of your property market value. In addition, your agent helps you negotiate, submits offers, and assists with a property due diligence. In my first deal, my agent even helped me to renegotiate the price on closing day. When you look for your real estate broker, try to choose the one with significant working experience of not less than five years. Your agent should possess good communication skills and be accessible during each day and at weekends. Try to avoid the agents who became too busy for you and were concentrating on more lucrative clients. Your agent should be *hungry* enough to earn their commissions and want to get new clients. It's important to find the realtors who have sufficient experience and are willing to work with investors; it requires a completely different approach and understanding of clientele. You should stop dealing with agents who don't understand your goals and needs.

Keep in mind that agents also prequalify you during your first meetings with them. They would like to be sure whether it's worth working with you. They want to check whether you are serious enough or just wasting their time. This is the one of the main reasons they are not enthusiastic about working with the beginner investors.

Experienced agents don't want to spend time educating them. To avoid that, you need to show the agent your determination and persistence. There is another point you need to keep in mind: many agents don't want to assist investors with buying the distressed properties at a low price due to low commission fees. Ensure them you will invite them again to sell this property in the future. If you remain happy with the first deal, you will purchase your next investment property through them.

The best way to find good real estate agents is to network with other investors active in your area. Don't miss any opportunity to talk to them by phone or during special investor events. If you succeed to establish a good rapport with them, you will probably get the referrals for other good professionals, such as contractors and property managers. Often, I also browse through real estate internet sites like Trulia.com and Redfin.com. While I search for a good deal online, I always notice the names of the listing agents related to each property I like. I constantly create a list of agents who I often meet online. It means they are very active in that market. Then I call them and set up a meeting. The final source to find good realtors is to call into the main offices of well-known brokerage companies like Re/Max, Keller & Williams, and Coldwell Banker. You should talk directly to the chief manager and ask to be introduced to their best available real estate agent. Tell them you want the agent with enough experience working with investors. In most cases, you will get the names of skilled professionals. The important thing, when you work with a real estate agent, is to constantly motivate them for an outstanding performance. Your real estate agent will be helpful for your business; you just need to push them to bring you new deals and take massive actions when buying new properties. That creates rapport and trust with your realtor.

How to Find Your Real Estate Attorney and CPA

Your real estate attorney is the second important member of your team. Personally, I assign such a high value to this professional because their importance to my real estate investment journey has been undeniable. If you make the right choice in finding an excellent attorney, in the end, he or she will help you save money. As soon as you expand your real estate empire, your attorney will also help you earn money. But first, you need to know how to find quality attorneys, then pre-select the best one and foster a good relationship with him or her, all before you even begin making offers. It costs you nothing to build a relationship with your lawyer from the beginning; it will only cost money if you use his or her services.

You will need your attorney for four main reasons/business areas: the first is when you create your legal structure. Your lawyer is responsible for all paperwork and will guide you through the pitfalls and nuances of incorporating your legal entity. I will touch on this subject in more detail in Chapter 6. Next, you'll need your attorney when you begin making offers. As soon as an offer is accepted, the contingency period comes in force. Your attorney should immediately work your contract out and, during this short period of between five and ten days, you'll be able to perform your due diligence of the prospect property. If you don't like that property, you can ask your attorney to legally withdraw from the deal. Critically, you are at risk of being sued by the opposite side if you fail to correctly complete all necessary paperwork. To avoid this messy outcome, I personally prefer to use my attorney in situations when I want to cancel my offer. If you like the prospect property, your lawyer will draft and arrange a fully executed contract and prepare the file for closing. And here, you'll employ your lawyer for their third task. He or she will also verify that your property is free of any liens. You may need to remind him or her about this important issue. In my case, my attorney ensured me that he never permits me to close on any property with any liens on it, and you should demand your attorney does the same! You should arrange for your attorney to represent you entirely during the closing. You don't need to be present during the process, and you can do other important things at that time. I will touch on this point in the chapter dedicated to closing. However, the most critical moment where a lawyer is necessary is during litigation. As many investors say, the question is not *if* somebody will sue you in the future; the question is *when*. However, when you have established the correct legal structure, umbrella insurance, and good lawyers who are standing by you one hundred percent and ready to fight for you, then the risk of litigation is not as scary. Moreover, the potential hazard of being sued shouldn't prevent you from investing in real estate.

In all the situations mentioned above that would prove hard to solve at a glimpse, the role of your lawyer is crucial. So, what criteria should you apply to selecting an excellent attorney that will allow you to sleep well thereafter? First, you should find a good local attorney. Since each state has its own laws, you need a lawyer well skilled in domestic legislation. The second condition is that your lawyer must have been in business for at least five years. He or she should also specialize in real estate and possess extensive knowledge in the field. Be sure to ask him/her about fees, because you need to understand and account for how much their services will cost you. Try to choose an attorney who does not charge you too much. Preferably, his/her firm has worked with a long list of customers, including clients with a smaller budget. So, you might expect their fees to be very competitive. Furthermore, your initial cases will likely not be complicated and require extra fees. Your lawyer should also be easy to communicate with, always be helpful, and be ready to advise you on any legal point. He should always protect and prioritize your interests. I also recommend finding a professional who has a great personality, which will ensure you are able to avoid many problems in future. Keep in mind that an excellent attorney should be an asset, not a liability.

How can you hire a good lawyer? I recommend googling your local bar association, which will provide referral services. You may also ask for referrals from your local real estate association and as you network with other investors. You may find them online (A list of useful online resources where you can find real estate attorneys is available on my book site, www.MakeItBigBelowTheBorder.com). I recommend you compose a list of ten local real estate attorneys. Call them one by one, and dedicate enough time to talk to each of them. Pose any and all prequalifying questions you have. Then, select the best three attorneys from your list. During your first trip to your target city, visit them all. This first meeting with your attorney is much more important than your previous call. It will begin to create rapport with your lawyer. He will notice that you are serious enough to come to his office and meet him personally. During this first visit, you should focus on your legal entity configuration because you will need to set up your company before you can begin. After your company (either an LLC or partnership) is created, you can commit yourself to a property transaction.

A Certified Public Accountant

Be sure your accountant specializes in real estate investments because it is important that your CPA understands the tax implications of real estate. An experienced CPA will know what questions to ask you and what to look for in your real estate financial documents. He will also be aware of any new rules and changes in state and federal tax regulations. As with your lawyer, you'll need to create a good level of rapport and communication with your accountant. Developing this kind of relationship will help immensely with saving money. To find a good CPA, ask your attorney for referrals. Typically, real estate lawyers, who have been in business for a long time, know good accountants with proven track records in assisting real estate investors. Some real estate attorney firms even provide accountant services for their clients. I personally prefer that my legal and accountant issues be solved by one company. This ensures both professionals have real estate good expertise and also facilitates coordination between them if I need their advice on the same question.

How to Find Your Lender

Building wealth in real estate is directly related to your ability to get financing. Borrowed money allows you to create financial leverage. You should find a way to purchase properties with relatively small amounts of your own money. Later, when the repair works are finished, you should apply for refinancing with the purpose to reimburse your initial construction loan and get your investment money back. While the refinancing can be relatively easy to get through the conventional loans, chances to borrow money for a property in need of repairs are not so certain. There are two options: the first one is the private money, which we will discuss in this chapter, in the section on how to find partners and investors. The second option is hard money financing.

Hard money financing is short-term loans with high-interest rates and additional points. These loans allow investors to buy properties that couldn't be purchased otherwise through traditional financing. Banks do not usually lend on properties that need repairs, and only loan on properties in good condition. However, hard money lenders look for the deals where investors increase equity by repairs. These lenders are licensed individuals and companies, and the name, *hard money,* doesn't mean that such a loan is difficult to acquire. In most cases, it is the opposite. Although they still require information about your income, available funds, and credit score, they base their approval on the potential of the property you are going to buy. If you have a great deal, you may get a loan from them without good credit and income that is difficult to prove. So, their first priority is to look at the property, and they want to know the after-repair value. To assess this, they send an appraiser to estimate the most accurate price. Knowing the ARV of your investment property, they propose financing based on 60% to 70% of the ARV. This ratio is also known as the loan-to-value or LTV. Their reason to lend 60% or 70% of LTV is that if a lender defaults on a loan, the hard-money lenders have enough space in the profit to justify the risk, i.e. their loan is secured enough by the property. Furthermore, they charge a high price for their money. In addition to the interest on the loan, they charge *points.* A point is 1% of the loan amount, and most hard-money lenders charge 2.5 to 4 points to originate the loan. The good news is that, in most cases, they will *roll* the points into the loan, which means you don't have to pay the points at the beginning and from your own money. Interest normally ranges from 13% to 18%. At first glance, this sounds unreasonable. However, hard-money loans are given for the short-term over a period between nine to twelve months. So, you won't pay too much interest in such a short time, and it doesn't seem so excessive when compared to your potential profit margins. In my opinion, if the investor can't afford to justify the points and high interest of a hard money loan toward a deal, maybe that deal is not really great. I use this principle to check the potential of any house I'm going to invest in. Nevertheless, I recommend using hard money with caution; it brings a significant risk. Keep in mind that you need to reimburse that loan in nine to twelve months. So, you have to be able either to repair and sell it with profit during that period or refinance it before the term, in which you should pay off your loan, ends. Another challenge is that the hard money lender will ask for your personal guarantee to secure the loan. However, today, even conventional banks ask for borrowers' personal guarantees. Everyone must decide for themselves whether these conditions are suitable for them. Terms and conditions for each particular loan depend on each hard money lender and how that loan is structured. So, my advice is to shop around and try to find the best hard money lender for your needs. I even recommend you create a list of them in your area with all their lending conditions; your next deals might be slightly different and then you have many options to select the best lender from your list. Another recommendation is to find the local hard money lenders in your city that have been in the business for at least ten years. These lenders know the neighbourhoods very well and can pre-approve your deal before charging you for an appraisal service. Many national lenders might not know the location of your property, and will need to send over an appraiser or an agent they trust. So, they may charge you some fees even before their preliminary approval.

The best way to discover hard money lenders is to search in Google combined with your city name. You may also get some contacts by calling mortgage brokers. Some of them can point you in the right direction. On my book website, MakeItBigBelow TheBorder.com, you can also find the list of hard money lenders who are lending money in some emerging markets throughout the country.

How to Find Your General Contractor

Finding the right general contractor is crucial. In fact, it's so significant that 50% of your success depends on this issue. Everyone has had some experience dealing with good and bad handymen. At first, it may seem a challenging and tough task to address and effectively communicate with construction people, but I've developed a specific system to pre-screen and work with them. Keep in mind that even if your first project doesn't go so smoothly, the next deals would be significantly easier. You just need to move on and follow the right strategy. These professionals are paid by the results of each profitable deal when they will start repairs, but before you should choose the best of them, close the deal, and get the financing for your repairs.

I prefer to hire a general contractor, rather than subcontractors, for many reasons. It's not easy to manage independent subcontractors who are each responsible for a different area of work, such as plumbing or painting, while living in another city or country. Furthermore, your lender will feel more comfortable knowing there is a professional, not just you, managing repair work, especially for complex projects with a budget of more than $50,000. Also, having a general contractor frees you from many liabilities and gives you a front person responsible for the whole repair project.

The best way to find a good general contractor is to collect referrals from other real estate investors. Consider joining various online real estate groups and platforms frequented by other investors; join a local real estate investment association and attend their meetings. Your real estate agent is another great source of information. In my practice, almost all realtors I have met are able to recommend at least two or three reliable contractors who have provided services for previous clients. You may also find contact information for general contractors, or handymen, online. You can search contractor databases on several websites, including Thumbtack, HomeAdvisor, or Angie's List. Your goal is to create a list of ten or twelve contractors. You won't need general contractors who work for huge and specialized projects, like new construction of 50-

unit apartment buildings because they and their management expertise are often expensive. You should also avoid subcontractors and handymen who are not properly licensed and insured for a general contractor job.

Your next job is to call at least ten or twelve general contractors from your list. You should pre-qualify them by asking the following questions:

- How long have they worked as a GC?
- Are they able to perform your project (renovation of 2-unit or 3-unit property), and how long will it take?
- How many workers are on their crew, and how many projects are they currently working on?
- Are they properly insured and licensed?
- Can they provide you with a copy of their license?

Most importantly, ask them for references from previous projects and clients, with phone numbers and addresses.

After you've preselected two or three of the GCs from your list, I strongly recommend you call and visit their previous jobs. Of course, your GC won't provide you with the contact information of dissatisfied clients but, even by visiting happy customers, you will learn a lot about your contractor's level of professionalism. You may notice the quality of finishes in kitchens and bathrooms and the quality of mechanical work on plumbing and heating systems. I suggest you dedicate one or two days for visiting the previous and the present projects of your pre-selected contractors. As I mentioned, you should choose at least three general contractors from your initial list.

Please keep in mind that, from their side, general contractors will also prequalify you as a potential client. In chapter 8, which is dedicated to managing repairs, I will flesh out how to create good rapport with your GC. Nevertheless, you will need to make a good first impression on the GC. Tell them you are not a retail client but that you are expanding your investment activity in their neighborhood and will be able to provide them with many projects if you are pleased with their work. Try to ask your GC questions about prices and timing for different types of work, including plumbing, HVAC, new kitchen installation, and any other examples that come to mind.

Ask your GC if he is ready to examine any property you are considering making an offer on. Will he be willing to provide you with estimates? This is important because that work is an essential part of your due diligence when you submit offers on certain properties. This aspect of his work is conducted without remuneration. Your GC knows he is going to be paid when he implements the repair works.

Finally, don't hesitate to ask your general contractor about his contacts with other professionals you will need to consult. He might be able to refer you to an excellent real estate agent, a property manager, or a home inspector.

How to Find Your Property Manager

Once you finish with repairs, you must choose your most appropriate exit strategy. You can sell the property and make money on the difference between selling and buying prices, or you can rent your property out. If you list your property for rent, you can then refinance it after a certain stabilization period. Normally, this period is six to nine months after filling all your units with good tenants. This strategy allows you to reimburse your initial investment and even stay in the black; but to succeed, you'll need the services of one more professional: your property manager. He or she is responsible for your property's operations: maintenance, rent collection, and finding new tenants. Nevertheless, many choose not to hire them, usually for two reasons. First, they want to save by not paying for property manager services, which average 7 to 10 percent of the total rental income. Second, they fear hiring an unfair and disreputable person that could lead to dire consequences, like unsatisfied and disappointed tenants, the rapid decline of a property due to improper care, and huge repair and maintenance costs. Even when faced with these risks, it's difficult to imagine your success in real estate without the services of the right, responsible property manager. We know many examples of prominent investors who successfully own rental properties located in other cities, and some even manage them from other countries. How can they achieve those results? The answer is simple. They found good, conscientious and reliable property managers. Thus, the initial task of each investor should be to find the same kind of experienced and knowledgeable professional. To do that, you need to learn where to look, what criteria you can apply to prequalify the best, and how to make them work for you as efficiently as possible. In each city across the country, you can find excellent property managers capable of providing their clients with high-quality and duly performed services at reasonable prices; ideally, your real estate deal should be so profitable that you can afford the valuable services of your property manager. They can help you avoid countless problems related to the management of your investment property, allowing you to sleep well and be completely focused on other important aspects of your real estate business. My task is to help you find and prequalify the best, and I've provided you with ideas for where to find them further in this paragraph. I've also dedicated a full chapter to property management, where you can get the blueprint for how to prequalify the best property manager, and a list of the questions you need to ask each candidate during your first meeting.

The first step to finding the ideal property manager is asking your real estate agent for referrals. A good agent should be able to provide you with a couple of names. You can also ask other investors investing in the same types of property in your neighborhood. In my opinion, their recommendations about this subject are the most reliable and accurate. Online, searchable databases are another great source of information. You can use multiple websites, including Yelp, Thumbtack, RentList.com, and AllPropertyManagement.com. Many have score systems that provide client reviews. Also, you may get the most valuable information in your search from the official sites of the Institute of Real Estate Managers (IREM) and the National Association of Residential Property Managers (NARPM). There you can research acting members of the NARPM and property managers certified by the IREM by typing the name of your city and property type. These experts have been trained by these organizations, which provides additional value and trust as you choose the best from among them.

Another important thing to remember: try to find a property management company whose primary focus is the same type of property you have or plan to invest in. Don't hire a company specializing in the commercial malls and big apartment complexes for your 2-unit property.

After creating a list of ten property management companies in your area, select the best three among them. Call each of these three companies and pose each of the pre-qualifying questions, which I also provide on my book's official website, www.MakeItBigBelow TheBorder.com. During your first trip to the city where you are investing, try to meet all three companies and set up personal contact with each of them. You may notice differences when meeting in person. During your second trip, meet with another three property management companies from your list. It's in your best interest to have access to as many real professionals as possible. Even if you choose the wrong property management company, your list of experts with whom you are in direct contact helps you deal confidently and even improve the situation by hiring a new company if things go too far.

How to Find Your Partner/Investor

Finding a partner for your first real estate deal is a great idea. As partners, you can do a lot more together than either could alone. Moreover, as a member of a partnership, you share all risk, all expenses, and all responsibilities for your mutual deal. This means a lot, believe me, especially during your first deal, when you'll likely face fear and uncertainty from your lack of experience. In addition, having a partner mobilises and encourages you—you have someone to whom you feel responsible for your actions. Together, your mutual business decisions and actions can be faster, sharper, and stronger. But not just anyone will do; you need to choose a good partner and avoid a bad one at all costs. Try to find a partner with a good personality and one who shares your vision, goals, and ethics. You may find a partner by attending special events or seminars for real estate investment or by networking online after creating a group, your own blog, or a social media page. Being proactive is the best strategy for finding them. Then, you need to be responsible to your partner. Try to make your partner glad they chose to go into business with you. Think about and protect his or her interests first, and show respect and be honest with them. While arguing, and you likely will argue, try to consider your partner's ideas in a positive way. Compromise; don't push him or her into only accepting your arguments and solutions.

Now, let's talk about using private investors for your first transaction. Private investors are also often referred to as private money lenders. They don't actively participate in the deal like partners would; instead they provide all the necessary funds for your deal. Private money lenders can be friends, parents, and other close relatives. Nevertheless, when you are a beginner, it's much easier to find a partner for your first transaction than a private investor, unless your loved ones have a strong desire to support you. Keep in mind that private investors first consider you and your experience and abilities, not your deal. I do not recommend any online or offline resources for finding investors for your first deal. In my opinion, there is no way to make a quick fortune in real estate. Like any business, you face a long tortuous journey toward your prosperity. Later, when you have succeeded and have created a big portfolio, cash flow, and a solid reputation, then people start believing and investing in your deals. At that point, it's much easier to bring in private investors' money but, even then, you need to be very accountable toward their money. Try not to put them at risk if you don't have a proven strategy and enough experience in this business.

Unite Everyone in Your Victorious Star Team

As you have likely noticed while reading this chapter, a great support team of knowledgeable professionals is the key to prosperity in real estate. Although they all have their own businesses, each individually makes an invaluable contribution to the growth of your real estate business. At first glance, it seems too complicated to meet and select so many team members right away, but you need to realize that you'll rarely need all of them on a regular basis and at the same time. And besides, these professionals receive compensation as a result of each profitable deal, so you won't need to pay upfront for most of them.

Your task is to create a cohesive and strong team. You need to continuously search for people whose methods, styles of work, and efficiency satisfy your expectations. Do not stop until you find them. Try to acquire these people by considering the recommendations of other professionals or, even better, from the advice of other investors. If these resources don't pan out, consult online resources, but give yourself enough time and effort to research and verify each specialist. It's crucial to meet and interview each potential team member in person after prequalifying the best candidates and considering their quality and the prices of their services. Try to effectively communicate and build rapport with all your team members from the onset. They should be your friends and understand that their success is your success.

Now, when you know how and who to choose for your winning team, it's time to act. Your hands are probably itching to seek out real deals, and I have good news for you: in the next chapter, we are going to talk about how and where to find houses with investment capacity.

Chapter 4

How to Find Properties with Investment Potential

"Know what you own, and know why you own it."
— Peter Lynch

In chapter two, you learned how to choose the right neighborhood, so you know the selection criteria now. It must be a suitable area with low crime and good schools. It is preferable to have amenities like hospitals, food stores, and shopping centers located within reach. You should choose the area with an inventory potential, i.e. the area where you can find a lot of good deals. The selling price for newly renovated homes must be high, and the average time on the market to sell such properties should not exceed six months. Your target neighborhood must show a great capability at any exit strategy when you want to sell your property or rent it. So, select the areas where the rents are high too. To find such neighborhoods online, use different websites like Trulia.com, Zillow.com, and Redfin.com. I will talk about how to do it efficiently in this chapter. Besides this, you can ask your real estate agent to advise you on the right areas and to send you the active listing of properties in those neighborhoods. So, let's talk about how to find great investment properties.

How to Preselect Properties From MLS Listings

When you ask your real estate broker to send you the active listing that covers your target area, you are likely to catch an immediate great deal. However, it doesn't happen often. You must be ready to wait because finding the right property takes time. Be patient and you will be paid in full. The information you get from MLS about your house indicates the selling price, average days on the market, year of construction, the number of bedrooms and bathrooms, square footage, and much more. You may see the photos of a property, if they are available; they give you an idea of the layout and the level of finishes. These pictures show you what condition the property is in now and what kind of repairs are needed.

There are a few points you should pay attention to when searching in MLS. First, look at the property exterior. Notice whether the facade of the building seems ugly or nice. Avoid houses that look hideous. Whatever repairs you do in the future, your customers will not like it. Also, my advice is to pick a brick home, if you have the choice between a brick and a vinyl house, as brick homes are valued more. The second important point is the number of bedrooms and bathrooms in your home. If you invest in two or three-unit properties, I suggest choosing houses with three bedrooms and one bathroom in each unit. Such a configuration is more attractive for families and has the potential for a higher rental income and ultimate selling price. If you aim for single-family houses, choose a property with more than four bedrooms and two bathrooms. The third factor is the property layout and interior square footage. Sometimes it's difficult to estimate how large rooms are in a house if you just view the pictures available on MLS. So, ask your real estate agent to check this information, especially for the master bedroom, kitchen, living, and dining rooms. If they are small and narrow, your property will be less attractive to your potential clients. The next point you must be careful of is the location of your property. It really is *location, location,* and, once again, *location*. I often use Google Maps to look around my property. I browse down the street from three to five blocks in each direction. It gives me enough information about the area, so I know quickly whether I want to buy a property in that location or not. I always notice the debris and dirt lying on the street, uncut lawns, or old rusty cars parked along the street. I also pay attention to any shops and restaurants that are nearby. I may even see the metal bars on the shop windows and doors on Google Maps. On the contrary, if I see malls, pizzerias, cafes, and fast-food restaurants in a five-block distance from my house, I make the decision to invest in the area. However, I still don't hesitate to ask the real estate agent for more information about the neighborhood. I want to know the reputation and whether people want to buy homes or rent in this district. Also, I ask about market trends for each area I want to invest in—whether they will go up, down, or stay stagnant. Another important point is to check whether the property has a garage or a parking lot, and whether it needs repairs or must be completely rebuilt. Also, you should know whether your property has an unfinished basement or a finished one. All this information is important for evaluating the repair cost and for estimating any expenses you can cut. Try to choose a house you like the most. Your intuition should tell you when it's the right decision. This is important because your potential buyers and tenants will likely have a similar impression of your property. They should love your house at first sight. So, your role as a visionary is to know how your property will look after renovation.

In the beginning, it takes time to gather all the necessary information about a property on MLS. I recommend not spending too much time observing. It comes with practice. You will feel comfortable after repeating your search several times. Then it takes no more than two or three minutes to know all you want about any property on MLS. This skill will help you to prequalify as many properties as you want on your short list. Remember, your task is to create a short list with preselected properties. It doesn't mean you should necessarily buy those properties. To make the final decision about the purchase, you should complete the initial information you have. The most important elements are the estimated repair costs and the after-repair value of the property, or the ARV. Repair estimates are provided by general contractors when you send them to look at your property. To define the ARV, real estate investors look for the property comparatives, which compare houses of similar style and square footage, with the same number of bedrooms and bathrooms, and in the same area. The best way is to match with newly renovated or newly inhabited houses sold in the same location within the past six months. Their selling price gives you an idea about the after-repair value of your investment property. It seems complicated at first glance but, in fact, it is very simple. By following my system, you will learn how to analyze properties in the fastest and most efficient way.

How to Use the Online Resources Effectively, Like Zillow, Trulia, Redfin, and Others

Although using the active and sold listings from MLS is a very accurate way to find and analyze properties, there are many other online resources to help real estate investors gather information about properties and the neighborhood where they are located. Most of these sites complement each other. You can find a lot of useful data about almost any house you want to invest in. Here, I will dwell on the information you can get with these sites.

Redfin.com

Redfin.com is the perfect map-based search tool for observing the active listings and comparatives in your target sector. Just type the name of your neighborhood in the Redfin.com search window, and you get the online map with all active properties there ready for sale. To get more precise information, you can apply a variety of filters: the minimum and maximum prices for sale; the number of bedrooms and bathrooms; property type; lot sizes; year of construction; and many other interesting things. If you want to receive comparatives for two-unit properties with three bedrooms and one bathroom in each unit and certain square footage, you just need to apply these criteria in the filter, and you will get accurate comparisons. It can save your time tremendously. It's possible to find some potential deals in the active listings as well. For this, you should apply your selective criteria in the filter windows.

I consider Redfin.com as one of the valuable sources of information about almost any property I am interested in, either active or sold. I can get the interior pictures, the number of bedrooms in each unit, property tax for the previous year, garage or parking lot availability, and information about rent and utilities paid by tenants. However, the most interesting is the property history, which indicates all selling and listed prices for at least ten consecutive years in the past; so, I can see what happened to my investment properties during that time. Often I am interested in looking at the history of newly repaired properties in my area; it gives me an idea how other real estate investors make money. I can find out: how much they paid for the property; how long it took them to renovate it; what price they sold it for; how long their renovated property was on the market; and the pictures of their renovation. You can learn a lot of information about how to do real estate business in your city if you use the comparatives correctly. Redfin.com is a good tool for this!

Trulia.com

Trulia.com is another great map-based search website. I usually use Trulia to look for active listings and comparatives. However, the most valuable is the information about the crime rate and assigned schools in the area. Crime indications help to find out how high, moderate, or low criminality is in your target neighborhood. For greater reliability, Trulia.com signals all recently reported offenses that occurred near your home. Furthermore, Trulia.com lists the assigned high, middle, and elementary schools in the area, together with the nationwide GreatSchool.org ratings based on test scores and other available data, including student academic growth and college readiness. The district performance data from GreatSchools.org includes ratings for schools on a scale from 1 to 10. A score from 7 to 10 means it is a good school, while a score from 1 to 4 may raise anxiety among parents who want to send their children to decent schools.

Another amazing point I like in Trulia is its Home Prices and Heat Map. It's useful when you want to compare different neighborhoods in your city and pick the best one. Trulia Heat Map provides investors with median selling and listing prices for each area in the cities around the country. You can also view a median rental price per bedroom, crime density, good school locations, demographics, and commute time. I highly recommend this service to all my readers as a source of valuable information. To have access to the Trulia Heat Map, just Google the name of your city and type *home price and heat map.*

Zillow.com

This is a very resourceful website. Most of the information here complements what you can find on Trulia.com and Redfin.com. It helps a lot when I need to prequalify many properties in a short time. Then, it is important to quickly get the approximate information about property value. Their home valuation, known as Zestimate, is based on the property information, market price, location, and other market conditions. I always consult Zestimate before proceeding with further detailed calculations regarding any selected property. Zillow.org also produces a Zestimate forecast, which is a property price prediction for one year ahead, based on current home and market data. However, I do not recommend relying on Zestimate as an accurate appraisal. There is an opinion that only a third of its value predictions are within five percent of the real sale price. Use it as a starting point for your property research.

Rentometer.com

Rentometer.com is another great online resource, providing investors with ideas about rental prices for their investment properties. After a trial period, there are some small fees to pay on a monthly basis. I highly recommend using this website for calculating the rent profit of your property. Rentometer.com compares all available data about all rented and listed properties in a certain neighborhood. As soon as you type the address of your investment property and numbers of bedrooms into the search bar, you will get more or less accurate numbers for your rental price. When it's time to buy the house, you can match numbers taken from Rentometer.com with those provided by a property manager who you have asked to prepare the rent appraisal of your property. Usually, property managers should provide you with two numbers: the rent amount for regular tenants and for Section 8 tenants. These two lease amounts could vary, and I will explain this in Chapter 9, which is dedicated to property management.

How to Find Properties From Craigslist and Other Sources

Craigslist is an online classified website where sellers create free advertisements to promote their properties for sale. In the section, *Housing*, just select *Real Estate–by owner*. Try to find properties in need of repairs with motivated sellers. You can find them by searching for specific keywords, such as *Motivated Seller*, or *Flexible Seller*. It could also be under *House Must Go*, or *Owner Desperate*. I never underestimate the importance of using Craigslist in my property research. Today, millions of people use Craigslist; the chances of finding a good deal there are pretty high.

Another way to find attractive properties is to use direct mail. There are many ways to generate leads, i.e. a list of potential sellers. At your county recorder's office, you can get the addresses of pre-foreclosed properties. Also, you may use an expired listing when agreements between the agents and the sellers have expired and the listing agents couldn't sell those houses. Another source is the list of the people who failed to pay their property tax. This list is available in your local tax assessor office. As soon you get this information, you can start a direct mail campaign. I recommend using handwritten letters printed on yellow paper. This type of marketing campaign generates higher responses because it draws more attention from potential sellers. Some can be distressed homeowners; they may feel frustrated about their personal situation. In your letter, you should genuinely let them know that you want to propose a solution to their problem. Mention to them that you are going to acquire the property in as-is condition, and there is no real estate agent commission. The direct mail campaign can bring you a lot of great deals over the years if you do it right.

Try to create networking connections with attorneys who specialise in pre-foreclosures, bankruptcies, divorces, and tenant evictions. Their clients might be your motivated home sellers, and attorneys can refer you to them. I recommend you target two types of lawyers: divorce lawyers, and attorneys who sue insurance companies. In most cases, their clients are already tired of lengthy litigation processes and are ready to get rid of their houses to end their emotionally devastating situation quickly. So, the toughest part of negotiations for convincing them to sell their homes has already been done.

Buying from wholesalers is another way to have access to great deals. However, I recommend using their services after you get some experience in real estate investing, or at least when you have already purchased a couple of houses. Wholesalers have no possibility to get financing for the great deals they found. Instead, they focus on finding distressed properties and proposing them to other investors. Usually, wholesalers charge between $3,000 and $5,000 for their services. The problem is that not all the deals they offer are necessarily good. You must be careful when selecting their homes. Before making any decisions, find out more information about the neighborhood and comparatives. In the next section, I will show you how to analyze houses and choose the best deals.

A Simple Way to Analyze Deals

Now you know where and how to find great investment deals. Through your real estate agent and other sources mentioned above, you will receive a huge number of properties waiting for your decision. Now you have to quickly make all necessary calculations on any property and select which ones are really worth it.

Make It Big Below the Border proposes one of the most efficient ways to analyze deals. It consists of two steps. I call the first one the *Preliminary Stage*, which helps you to create a list of interesting properties using online resources. During the next detailed *Diligent Stage*, you need to make more accurate calculations and consider all the specifics of your preselected houses. The good news is that you should not perform a diligent step before submitting your first offer. First, you should know in advance what kind of property you are looking for. Is it a single-family home or two-unit property? You should set the strict parameters of your search. Otherwise, you will be lost in research. It is also important how many bedrooms and bathrooms you expect in your investment property. If you follow my strategy, your target is a two-unit property with three bedrooms and one bathroom in each unit. (I've already explained this point in chapter 1.) Also, you need distressed houses requiring major repairs; otherwise, you won't be able to quickly increase the value of your investment property.

So, the formula to calculate an affordable purchase price for a distressed property is the following:

Purchase price (PP) = 65% * After Repair Value of your property (ARV) - Cost of Repairs.

It is a very simple formula. The point is how to find the ARV and repair cost for each preselected property.

So, let's start with ARV. This is the price of your house once it's fixed up. Choose three properties you like the most from your list of properties. Send them to you real estate agent and ask to prepare the comparatives for these three properties. Your agent should know how to prepare them. Each comparative must meet the following criteria: newly renovated properties or houses in really good condition; sold within the last six months and in the same neighborhood as your property; have the same number of bedrooms and bathrooms, and almost the same square footage; and if your target property has other features like a garage or a finished basement, the comps should have the same specifics.

My only advice is not to overwhelm your broker with such work. That's why many brokers don't like to work with beginner investors; they will have to do a lot of unpaid work before the first deal happens.

In my opinion, you will only need the assistance of your agent to find ARV comps for your first deal. When you learn how to search ARV online, through Trulia.com, RedFin.com, and Zillow.com, you can just apply the same criteria mentioned above in your selection filters. Experience comes with practice after you repeat your pursuit several times.

Then you need information about your repair costs, which is specific for each distressed property. Here we apply some rough assumptions; let's call them the rule of thumb. If your property needs some cosmetic updates, a very rough estimate is somewhere between $15,000 and $20,000 per unit. So, a two-unit property will need about $30,000–$40,000 for some light repair work. If we are talking about extensive work, including the installation of new mechanical, electrical and plumbing, new kitchen, new bathroom, and other similar tasks, the price range is between $40,000 and $45,000 per unit. These numbers involve labor and materials costs. I want to underline that these numbers are not final, and may vary from state to state across the country. These numbers just give you some preliminary ideas about repairs.

While looking through the description and pictures of the property on MLS, you may notice what repairs are needed; so, it helps you to figure out the preliminary list of works. To get a rough idea about the renovation budget, you should talk to construction workers and investors in your city and ask them how much it costs to repair each item from your list. Of course, you can obtain more accurate information later when you send a general contractor to make work estimates in your house. I just want to warn you not to ask him to look at properties each time you find them on MLS. They will just get frustrated preparing their estimates several times for you with no result. You have a reason to send your contractor only when you submit an offer. It sounds serious when you tell him: "Hi, John! I just put an offer on one property. Could you look at it and tell me how much it will cost to renovate it?" Don't worry that you do not have estimates before submitting an offer. You have enough time to withdraw from the transaction even after the offer is accepted!

To make a quick decision about repair costs for each certain property, you just need to apply *the rule of thumb.* By relying on these preliminary assumptions, you can calculate the purchase price you can afford. If your numbers match the formula, you can put an offer on that property. If you decide to make the detailed analysis before submitting your offer, you may lose the deal, because scrutinizing information about houses takes time and good deals do not stay for long. Your competitors will take this chance. Don't be afraid to make mistakes. These skills to quickly define great deals in real estate come with practice.

All You Need to Know About Submitting Your Offer

As I mentioned in the previous section, my system has a goal to make your whole investment process easy, enjoyable, and efficient at the same time. While starting to analyze investment properties, you may find a few homes where the numbers match the formula. Then you ask your real estate agent to put an offer on them. Today, real estate brokers prepare offers in online formats with an electronic signature. You can sign your offer from your smartphone even if you are in a different part of the world. However, you should still pay attention to some major details while you sign the offer, which is officially called a Residential Real Estate Contract:

Your Purchase Price. Always verify the price. Your realtor can mistakenly enter another number.

Initial Earnest Money. This is your deposit money, which you should transfer to the seller during the 2–3 business days after the Date of Acceptance. (Date of Acceptance is the day your offer will be accepted by the seller.) Normally, it is about US$1,000. The Earnest money deposit can be higher in the case of bank sales, like foreclosure or a short sale.

Closing Date. Usually, the closing date is fixed one month after the offer acceptance. It can be postponed by both parties in the case of unforeseen circumstances or when one side wants to prolong financial or attorney contingencies. I suggest always arranging such prolongations with the assistance of your attorney.

Mortgage Contingency. If you are paying cash, you do not need a mortgage contingency. This is a significant competitive advantage. Any sellers prefer to avoid the significant loss of time due to the risk of the buyer to obtain the financing. You may even negotiate a better purchase price just because you are paying cash. However, you should stipulate enough time for mortgage contingency if you plan to get a mortgage to acquire the property.

Tax Proration. Real estate taxes shall be 100% prorated for the full tax year. That means the seller should pay the full year's real estate taxes at the time of closing. At closing, this tax proration is important because it will be credited to you; sometimes this can cover a major part of your closing expenses and fees.

Attorney Review Contingency. Usually, this is fixed within five business days after the date of the offer acceptance. It is the most important contingency because you can use this time to send your general contractor to estimate repairs and to get a CMA from your agent. Based on your decision, your attorney can either approve or disapprove the contract, or propose modifications or suggested changes. Sometimes your general contractor may find some serious problems in the property, and this will significantly increase your renovation budget. So, you have a chance to withdraw from the deal in such a case. Also, you may propose to decrease the price or ask the seller for credit at closing to cover your unforeseen expenses. Keep in mind that minor repairs and routine maintenance of the property cannot be considered in this situation.

The seller agrees to leave the property in *broom clean* condition, and all personal stuff shall be removed at the seller's expense prior to the closing date. I had an experience when acquiring my first property in Chicago; I had to order a full dumpster to clean the property, and that cost me about $4,000. Thanks to this clause, I was able to credit this amount from the seller at the closing date.

Title. The title of the property must be cleared of any liens, encroachments, and any unpermitted exceptions. The seller has full responsibility to remove all these items and be insured against any court-ordered removal of the encroachments. In other words, instruct your attorney not to let you close a property that has any liens on it.

In addition to the offer, your real estate agent will ask you for two additional important papers: proof of funds (it can be your bank statement for the last three months) and your corporate papers, like the article of incorporation or the operating agreement, confirming your right of signature.

Additional Formula – How to Calculate Whether Your Property Can Bring You Positive Rental Cash Flow

In *Make It Big Below the Border,* I propose the strategy of renting your property to good tenants. So, you need to know whether your property has the potential to provide you with enough positive cash flow from the rent. To calculate your potential rental income, you can use the NOI formula (the Net Operating Income from the rent). We compute NOI by subtracting the vacancy rate and all expenses, except mortgage payments, from the Gross Rent Income. (Gross Rent Income is the annual sum of the rents collected from your property after renovation.) NOI shows you the net profit you get from renting your property, if you do not take any mortgage out and pay cash in full at purchasing.

NOI = Gross Rent Income - Vacancy Rate - All the Expenses

The expenses include real estate tax, property insurance, maintenance, contract services, and property management fees.

Expenses do not include utility costs because I assume that your tenants will pay them for you. You just need to be sure that electric, gas, and water meters are installed for each unit in your property. Management fees could be different in different areas, but I prefer to assume it at 10% of Gross Income. I also expect 10% of Gross Income for the property maintenance, taking into consideration that all major repairs would be done before you rent your property. I will talk about expenses in detail in the chapter dedicated to property management.

Then, ask your real estate agent to provide you with information about property tax, insurance, utility costs, and current contract services costs. Also, ask them about the situation with vacant properties in your area. It is crucial information. Try to invest in the areas where the vacancy rate is between 5 and 10%. If it is higher than 15%, I recommend finding another neighborhood.

So, now you know how to calculate the NOI for your property, which is helpful to figure out many other financial parameters of your property investment. One of them is the *capitalization rate*, also known as the CAP rate. This financial variable shows whether your property is profitable or not. Furthermore, the CAP rate allows you to financially assess many houses simultaneously if you need to choose from a large number of homes offered on the market.

CAP Rate = Net operating income (NOI) / (Purchase price of the property + Repair Cost)

To compute the CAP rate, you should divide the NOI by the sum of the property's purchase price and repair costs. Usually, the CAP rate formula is useful for an accurate calculation of commercial properties with five units and more. In our case, this method just gives us an idea whether the rent can cover all the expenses or not. My recommendation is to withdraw from deals where the CAP rate is less than 0.08 (or 8%). This rule works for decent neighborhoods. In high-crime areas, the CAP rate can reach as high as 20% because of the low cost of houses that are unable to achieve high rents. However, this is not the sole reason to avoid buying properties there. Your expenses, including maintenance, minor repairs, and property management, together with high vacancy rates, can reach staggering highs. So, invest in decent areas and purchase properties with a CAP rate higher than 8%. If a property has less than 8 %, abandon the deal and go for another one.

What Else Not to Forget After Submitting an Offer: CMA and Property Layout

There are two points you should ask for from your agent and general contractor after you have submitted your offer: Comparative Market Analysis (CMA) and the property's layout. As I mentioned before, the CMA provides you with the more accurate comparatives. This mini-review with business analysis of your property shows you correct numbers related to the value of your home after repairs (the ARV). Ask your agent to prepare the CMA only after you submit an offer. Otherwise, you will bother your real estate agent with wasted work.

To get the property's layout, just ask your general contractor to take pictures of the inside of your house when they go to make their estimates. This information is important. It helps you to figure out the potential of your property regarding volumes and spaces in bedrooms, kitchen, and other areas of your property. Before accepting the offer, you should know whether the bedrooms, kitchen, and living room are spacious enough. Don't buy houses with very small and narrow lodgings.

Also, ask your general contractor to point out and to take pictures of all the defects in the property: missing plumbing; missing copper wiring; damaged ceramics or broken kitchen cabinets. Don't be scared when you see some of them in the pictures. This information about damages in your house should not change your decision for acquiring the property. On the contrary, you need to learn how to use it for renegotiating the price. This is the fascination of making lemonade from a lemon! So, I will tell you how to create this magic and successfully negotiate in the next chapter.

Chapter 5

How to Negotiate and Make Due Diligence

"Let us never negotiate out of fear.
But let us never fear to negotiate."
– John F. Kennedy [Inaugural Address, January 20, 1961]

When I started my first deal, I thought negotiating the purchase price and performing the due diligence of the property would be difficult after my offer was accepted. Guided by this concept, I tried to make the detailed analysis for every property before submitting an offer on it. Eventually, I lost many good deals, wasting the time of my realtor. Later, I realised all I can do at this stage is make a rough evaluation. I learned, from the moment of the offer acceptance, I could have access to detailed information about the property, and there is enough time to make an accurate inspection and renegotiate the deal. Now, I use this occasion to focus on gathering correct numbers and all necessary data about the property! It is also an excellent opportunity to bring to the table all newly discovered facts, and pull down the purchase price.

What Questions to Ask to Get a Clear Picture About Seller Motivation

By searching the properties through MLS, it's difficult to find the motivation of the sellers, due to the absence of direct contact with them. I always ask my real estate agent to obtain as much information as possible about the seller's reasons, from the moment we receive the counter-offer. I ask my agent to research why the sellers want to sell. What is important to them in each case? To close faster or to be paid by cash? I even insist my agent inquire on the seller's side about all possible problems related to the property. This information can help me and my contractors pay attention to all those possible issues. In rare cases, you may have an occasion to meet the homeowner in person during your first visit to the property. You can learn enough about his motivation by listening to his story and asking him questions, while not infringing on the interests of your agents.

If you use other resources to search the properties, like direct mail campaign and Craigslist, you can negotiate with homeowners directly. Then, finding the right approach toward homeowners is of paramount importance. The best way is to solve their problem. You are sincerely helping to resolve the difficult situations the seller is facing. You can come to this by asking the right questions. They must be open-ended questions, encouraging the sellers to tell you their story. It makes the sellers feel an emotional tie with you that will help you build rapport with them. In addition, it gives you a deeper understanding of their motivation. So, your chances to buy property at a discounted price will grow. Here are the most important questions to ask the sellers:

Why are you selling? They may have a specific reason for this. Your task is to find out and give them an alternative solution to get what they want in exchange for a price reduction. The seller may need to pay urgent medical bills or need to pay attorney fees for filing probate on an inherited house. Try to help people. Sometimes you need to find a creative way to solve their problem.

When do you want to close? If it matters, you can propose to close in 30 days, instead of 45. You may exclude the financial or inspection contingencies from your purchase agreement, just to facilitate the deal.

What do you plan to do if the property doesn't sell? It's important to create a clear picture in his head about consequences of such a situation. You may observe by the seller's reaction whether he is ready to accept your proposal. The seller may avow he needs to get rid of the property soon. That means you should propose an idea to speed up the closing. He could also tell you he is not in any rush and may postpone the sale for the next year. So, you know he is not motivated enough.

Tell me what's going on with the property? Look carefully at the seller's body language. Is he telling you the truth, saying everything is okay with the property? Normally, people will tell you the real situation; they know you will find out after inspection.

Have you missed any mortgage or tax payments? This may be one more reason to negotiate the price. This could be quite a serious motivation for the seller.

The more you listen, the more likely they will tell you everything you should know. Even if buying properties through real estate agents, you need to ask the same questions and negotiate the same way as if they were the homeowners. Real estate agents find it helpful when you provide your reasoning. Usually, they use your arguments with sellers, which makes their job easier.

Once you understand the seller's motivation, you need to be prepared with a quick and sometimes creative idea about how to help them. It comes with practice. If the sellers are going through a divorce, you can come up with an idea to close quickly. If the seller has health issues, you may propose to buy the property with cash and offer your assistance with relocation. If the motivation is to find better schools for their children, you may refer them to a good agent who can help find a property in a decent neighborhood with a great school. We should help people by offering something valuable to them and creating a win-win situation. Only with this approach, you can get favourable deals!

Your Negotiation Tactics From the Moment You Receive a Counter-Offer

When you define a price to put in your offer, first look whether the real figures match the formula. As you may remember, your maximum allowable offer is a difference between 65% of the after-repair value and the repair cost. So, this is the top limit; above that, your deal stops being a good one. Remember, the maximum allowable offer is just a simple indication, helping you to be aware of not crossing this line during the negotiation. You can only put this price in your offer in a hot market. However, during the stagnant real estate market, my advice is to put your price between 5% and 7% below this limit, depending on the situation. So, stand at your price and submit it with your offer.

Sometimes you may have no answer from the seller. Later, your agent informs you that the seller has accepted a better offer from one of your competitors. My advice is to forget the deal. Let someone else profit from it. If you start the race to drop the price, there is the risk of buying a bad asset with no profit for you. It's better to look for another good deal. There are a lot of them around. However, you may keep watching this property, occasionally. Look at how much it sells for. It gives you a clear vision of current trends in your market.

The situation changes once you get a counteroffer. The seller shows up with his price. Sometimes the first reaction is to split the half and agree on that price between both parties. Here, in *Make It Big Below the Border,* I don't recommend you negotiate this way. Instead, I suggest you make small reductions toward the seller's proposal. What does it mean? Let's say you put in an offer for $88,000 on a property that is listed on MLS for $98,000. You have made your calculation, and the max allowable price is $93,000. That means, above this price, the deal ceases to be profitable. The difference between the seller's price and your offer is $10,000. The first step is to receive a counteroffer. The seller put down his price for $95,000, showing his or her willingness to close the deal. As your second step, you move toward the seller's position for 15% of the difference between the original seller's price and your offer; in our case, it is $1,500. Your new proposal is $89,500. Meanwhile, this looks like it is based on strong mathematical calculations. The seller comes back to you, proposing $93,000. He insists it is his last proposition. So, you implement step three, moving up to another 15%. Your offer is now $91,000. You suggest closing the deal in 30 days. If the seller accepts your proposal, you will buy the house for $2,000 less than your maximum allowable offer. The idea is to move up by small reductions. Remember, it happens without direct contact between you and the homeowner, through the assistance of two real estate agents, representing each side. So, at this stage, you should be tough.

Use all information you may have during the negotiation favorably. In my last deal, the seller didn't want to drop the price, arguing the appraisal his agent had provided him was 25% higher than his selling price. I reminded him, despite such a high evaluation, his property couldn't sell in 250 days for a much lower price. You need to be well-prepared with your arguments.

Insist on sending your general contractor to assess the repair work. It's crucial to get your contractor's estimate when the offer is accepted. There is an important rule. When you get clear information from your general contractor, always renegotiate the price. He might find some unexpected problem. His estimates may also exceed your preliminary expectations. It's in your interest to identify how much it would cost you. Then, ask the seller to lower the price by that amount. There is a chance the seller may feel offended. To improve the situation, I recommend writing a letter directly to the seller and asking your agent to deliver it. In this letter, explain you have no intention of offending the seller. You still want his property. You just want to buy it for the right price. Explain in the letter why you dropped the price. The second argument you may use is that due to the high selling price and increased construction budget, the bank won't finance the deal. The same problem will appear, no matter who the buyer is. If the seller wants to cancel the transaction, he has the risk of not finding another buyer for a long time. Ensure him you will close relatively fast. Tell him the exact day you would like to close. If you put your offer in at the beginning of April, and you intend to close the transaction in 30 days, tell the seller you are closing at the beginning of May. It's important to create a clear picture in his head that, in May, he will get money from the property selling.

Ask For Credits at Closing. Often,
It Works Better Than Dropping an Offer Price

During renegotiation, especially when your general contractor has found some serious problem, your first reaction is to drop the price. Here, in *Make It Big Below the Border,* I suggest you handle this situation differently. It works remarkably when you take a loan to acquire the property. To illustrate the point, I'll give you an example with purchasing a 2-unit property for $110,000. Let's say a bank will loan you 70% of the purchase price. Your down-payment should be around $33,000. During the inspection, your general contractor has found something serious that will increase your repair budget by $12,000. Now, your goal is to explain the situation to the seller and force him or her to accept this price reduction. After lengthy discussions, the seller will lower the price by $10,000. Instead of changing the price, you will ask him for the same amount, credited at closing. What does this mean? In the closing statement, you ask the seller to reflect this amount as a credit to you. (The closing statement is one of the documents you need to sign during the closing. It presents every cost involved in the transaction. It might have different names, like a master statement or a closing settlement, depending on the state you are investing in.) So, asking the seller for the $10,000 credit at closing allows you to deduct it from your downpayment, i.e. from $33,000. Now, you will pay $23,000, instead of $33,000, as the down-payment. What happens if you just drop the price, with no credit? The selling price is $110,000. You will lower the price to $100,000 because you will have agreed to $10,000 for reduction. So, your downpayment will be $30,000. However, in the first scenario, you will pay only $23,000! Do you see the difference?! So, my advice is to ask for credits during negotiation. Seasoned investors use a few other tricks to significantly decrease a cash down-payment at closing; it also works with purchasing apartment buildings with more than five units. If you are interested, you may visit the book website, www.MakeItBigBelowTheBorder.com, where I share this information as a free bonus.

Due Diligence. Send Your General Contractors to Make Their Estimates

The due diligence is the most important part of the property acquisition. It is a simple process that should be done properly. Ignoring the due diligence causes significant problems for novice investors and their investments due to the risk of losing big sums of money at the end. Start your due diligence by sending three of your general contractors to make their estimates on your house. In the previous chapter, you learned how to create a short list of contractors. So, it's time to use this list. You will select the best three GCs and remember another three professionals. I will explain why to remember another three builders little bit later. So, you will call the first three contractors from the list, asking them to bid for your construction project. Ask whether they want to participate. You will tell them you will call again in a few days, informing them of the date and time when they can go see the property. You will provide them with the address, a brief description of the property, and what kind of repairs you expect to be done. Then you will call your real estate agent, asking him/her to arrange a showing to your contractors. Let your agent organise the showing just after you get a counter-offer! Explain to your agent it's an open bid, and all contractors should come at one time in the same day! Some contractors may refuse to estimate the property at the same time as competitors. You should respect that. But it doesn't prevent you from scheduling one visit after another. Ask your real estate agent to be there during the showings and to take pictures or videos of the inside of the property.

There are three essential things you should pay attention to when you inspect the property. First, ask your contractors about all serious problems the property might have. It could be a foundation issue, sloping floors, and huge fire damage. The second point is the total cost for renovation. It comes with renewing HVAC, kitchen, bathrooms, and other items in the property. The last point is how long it will take to make repairs. Insist on getting answers for these three points. The good contractors will send you the list of work to be done, also known as a Contractor's Proposal or Renovation Construction Budget. It describes work, material and labour costs, and time of implementation. One or two contractors may not appear during property showings. Some won't even inform you about that. The others will find reasons not to come, and will ask you to postpone the showings until the weekend. I consider it an excellent opportunity to abandon irresponsible and undisciplined contractors. This is when the list of general contractors helps you. Just pick up the other three builders and call them. Your goal is to create a list with as many good contractors on it as you can. Remember, in this business, you are not stuck if you have many options.

Another important professional you require for your property due diligence is an inspector. My strong advice is to employ his services during your first two or three real estate transactions until you get enough experience. Ask your real estate agent to provide you with a list of reliable professionals. To select the best one, you will use the same criteria as those you will apply to look for other professionals in your team. Find a competent expert with at least ten years of experience in the field, and who is properly licenced and insured. Look carefully at the summary of his report. It's where all the problems are collected. If you find a huge mechanical problem in your property, cancel the deal and look for another one. Finally, learn when to send the inspector to the property. It's wasteful to hire an inspector each time your offer is not yet accepted. His service could cost between $400 and $500 for an inspection of 2-unit properties, and it varies from one state to another. So, you will send the inspector only after the acceptance of the offer. Usually, you are in time with the inspection contingency term that allows you to perform the property inspection in the five days after the offer is accepted.

Create Your Own Scope of Work. It's Not a Difficult Task

To understand numbers provided by the general contractors in their estimates, have your own template for evaluating repair costs. It's a simple price-specification list in which you enter the data about the repair cost on each type of construction work. However, don't forget repair costs vary throughout the country, so you need a separate specification for each area you want to invest in. Think about preparing this price specification before you submit your offers. As soon as your list of general contractors is ready, send a standard sample of price specification to every contractor and ask them to fill it in, either by hand or digitally. You can tell them it is the most important test by which you will select the best candidates for your project. You need to prepare this standard sample in advance. It's easy to make. It just depends on your determination and your ability to communicate effectively with construction people. Below, I give an example for a few types of work.

Task	Unit	Cost of Materials	Labor Cost	Time
Basic Carpentry	Per hour	$25	$25	*
Install Exterior Door	Per door	$250	$50	2 hours
Install Interior Door	Per door	$60	$30	1 hour
Replace window	Per-window	$150	$70	*

The sample of this specification with a list of work, can be found on the book website, www.MakeItBigBelowTheBorder.com, as a free bonus. Remember, prices for materials and labour costs are different in neighbourhoods across the country. They might even differ among different contractors working in the same city. So, on our website, you will find a sample to be filled in by your construction people.

Another important point follows. When you send the general contractors to see your property, ask them to prepare the repair estimates, indicating material and labour cost for each item by room. I mean, they should specify each type of work to be done in every bedroom, kitchen, bathroom, living room, and everywhere on the property, interior and exterior. It helps you to create your own *scope of work.* Later, you will incorporate this scope of work as an essential part of your construction contract. It also helps you to compare the estimates coming from different contractors, as an *apple-to-apple.* Based on this information, you can select the best professionals for your project, whose prices and performance level meet your expectations. Also, you will get the price list for almost all main types of construction work specific for your target neighbourhood. Making it once avoids you having to come back to this point for your next real estate investments.

Your Final Decision: Accept a Counteroffer or Quit the Deal

From the moment you receive a counteroffer, I recommend you transfer your file to your attorney. You may also ask your real estate agent to do that for you. Your attorney will search the document thoroughly and will warn you if something is wrong. You should receive three estimates from the general contractors participating in the bid. Now, you have a clear picture of your repair cost and the main items you need to fix in the property to bring it to normal condition. You also get the comparative market analysis (CMA) from your agent. You are aware about the accurate after-repair value for your property. You put all these numbers in the formula again and decide whether you need this deal. If the numbers don't match, you have two options—either cancel the deal or renegotiate the price. Also, abandon the deal in the case of serious construction problems, such as a big crack in the structure, sloping floors, heavy fire damage, or flooding. Where you do not have severe construction problems, my recommendation is not to drop the deal, but renegotiate the price. Decrease the price until the deal becomes profitable again. If you cancel the deal two or three times in a row, you are creating an image of a bad performer, and your agent will not be willing to do business with you again. Instead, send him all three estimates, the inspection report, and your calculations as proof of your serious intention. Now, it's up to another side to decide. By doing this, you will strengthen your reputation as a professional real estate investor.

When your offer is accepted, immediately send the contract to your attorney for further execution. From this day, known as *acceptance day,* all provisions of the offer, including all contingencies, are coming to force. It's is crucial you perform these actions starting on acceptance day:

- Arrange all pending issues with your lender before the deadline for your financial contingency expires.
- If you didn't get your repair estimates in time, send your general contractors to the property.
- Arrange the property inspection by a licenced inspector.
- Get your inspection report ready before the inspection contingency term expires.
- Ask your real estate agent in writing where to send the earnest money, e.g., the seller's escrow account.
- Arrange your earnest money transfer within one week.
- Ask your agent to provide the copy of all documents about the property, like utility bills, insurance, and property taxes, for the last 2 years.

If you are not in time to prepare your financing or get the inspection report, you can extend the contingency terms by making necessary amendments in the offer. Ask your agent; he or she knows how to arrange that.

Also, you need to request another professional from the list you prepared when you were creating your team. I'm talking about a property manager. You may remember, we assumed you are renting your property after renovation. So, you will invite two property managers from your list to see your property. You need to know how much your property can be rented for after renovation. Besides their comments and recommendations about the property, they provide two important indications: the rent for regular tenants and the rent for Section 8 tenants. We will talk about Section 8 later, in the chapter dedicated to property preparation for Section 8 tenants. Usually, rent payment for Section 8 is higher than for regular tenants. I advise you to compare these numbers with online data from Rentometer.com. If the numbers differ, ask your property manager to explain. Information about the potential rent payments can give an idea about the future cash flow of your property.

The next steps any real estate investor should implement before closing day are of paramount importance for your investment. These steps can also lead to a lot of stress and aggravation if not done properly. Most beginners have a lot questions about what to do on the day of closing. So, in the next chapter, you will find solutions to everything that precedes and happens on closing day. Applying this knowledge makes your future property purchases an enjoyable experience for you and your partners.

Chapter 6

How to Close

"Success is where preparation and opportunity meet."
– Bobby Unser

In this chapter, I will inform you about the steps to be properly prepared before closing on your property, during and immediately after closing, and before you start construction on your new property. Timing is crucial to make sure the elements for a successful closing are set. Doing them correctly protects against many problems occurring and makes all your actions efficient for your closed deals. So, here we learn about what happens from the minute the seller accepts your offer and you have chosen your general contractor for the project.

Prepare Your File for Lender Approval

When it's time to decide how to finance your first deal, my recommendation is to buy it with cash. I will explain why this approach facilitates your first-time purchase. Earlier, in chapter 3, I mentioned hard money loans. Unfortunately, most banks and lending institutions will not lend you money to buy a house needing extensive repairs. Banks look at a damaged property as an asset with an enormous liability problem. So, the only choice to bring financing in the deal is hard money loans or private financing. However, many beginning investors have no access to private money. Even bringing hard money to your first deal might be problematic; most hard money lenders look seriously at your previous experience as a real estate investor. Even the financing terms may be tougher for the novice. One thing is for sure; your file consideration will take a lot of time, and there is the risk you will not be in time with your financing. The absence of US residency can cause significant delays too, which is not good news for my fellow Canadians. Despite some hard money lenders announcing they provide money within 7–10 business days, the reality is much more complicated. Therefore, I recommend buying the first deal with cash and then drawing a construction loan from a hard money lender. You may also find a partner, bring him in on your deal, and share half of your contribution to the cash purchase.

The good news is, when you take a construction loan, the hard money often provides financing that covers 65% of the total cost of construction and purchase price of your project. So, there is no difference, whether you take the hard money loan initially to buy the property or receive it later, after purchasing it with cash. In both cases, the total loan amount is the same. Lenders will not finance over 65% of the construction work and the purchase price, anyway. However, it will be much easier for a hard money lender to finance your transaction when the property is already acquired by you. So, bring your cash to purchase the property; then, you will take a hard money loan, part of which will cover 65% of your purchase price. It's worth mentioning that it will be much easier to borrow the money for your next deal; you will create a good rapport with your hard money lender during your first transaction.

However, if you borrowed the hard money for the purchase of your first investment property, you must do the following things:

At the time of getting a counteroffer, contact the top five hard money lenders from your short-list. As I recommended in chapter 3, you need to know the borrowing conditions of each lender and select those whose conditions satisfy you.

Prepare a single message with a description of your deal and send it to all selected lenders. It should include the address of the property, photos of the exterior and interior, purchase price, and the comparative market analysis prepared by your agent. Inform them you will send them the repair work estimates in 2–3 days.

Then you will receive the lender's application forms to fulfil. Usually, it comprises three parts:

- Property approval application form. Fill out all the information about your property and provide a brief description of your project.
- Investor's Personal Financial Statement. Here, they are asking you to provide personal information about your financial situation: assets, liabilities, income, and expenses.
- Information about your General Contractor. This application, you are sending to your GC to fill in. Inform your lender you are still bidding the repair work. You provide the general contractor the application when you select a winner. If the lender insists on receiving this form, ask all your bidders to fill out this form.

Your final goal is to obtain a financial approval letter from your lender. Getting such written proof, you make your seller more confident in doing business with you. It makes it easier for you, as well, to renegotiate the deal after property due diligence. Then, you keep pushing your lender for your financing to be ready on the closing day. If you have delays with your lender, you will ask your real estate agent to prepare an amendment to the purchase contract with an extension, and send it to the seller. Usually, it will cause no objections from a seller if delays are not too long.

What to Ask Your Attorney Before Closing

After the acceptance of your offer, there is another important stage. It's a legal due diligence, which should be performed by your lawyer. The results of this legal inspection will be reflected in the *attorney review letter*, which your attorney should prepare for the seller's side. Before sending the letter to the seller, your lawyer will provide a copy for your review and approval.

Before the legal due diligence, I recommend you check the Building Violations online and the Building-Related Court Actions on your future property. This information is easy to find in your city or county website. It clarifies if your property has any major problems with the city or county authorities. The execution of the qualified legal inspection must be done by your attorney. A great legal professional knows what to check and at which moment to start the inspection. A great attorney will tell you about all legal issues your potential property may have. He will tell you if these issues have a major significance and which actions you need to take to avoid them. Finally, you will have a clear idea if you need to cancel the deal or proceed.

Usually, your lawyer has five days for attorney review, as stated in the offer provision. You still can withdraw from the deal if your attorney finds something serious during these five days. Here, he will issue and deliver to the seller's attorney a termination notice stipulating your contract is null and void. He will charge you a small fee for this service. I always prefer to pay his fee than to settle this problem myself. There is a big chance I will do it wrong, and the seller's side may consider my refusal as invalid. They can even sue me after the purchase contract terms expire, forcing me to buy their property on unfavourable terms.

Next, I want to tell you what is included in the legal due diligence. Generally, your attorney knows what to do. It is his area of expertise. However, I want you to know about it too. The first thing you need to tell your attorney is, under any circumstances, you don't want to buy the property with an unclear title. He will review the sequence of the property ownership. He will tell you if any lien is on your property. He will seek any judgements and trespasses that might touch on your property. Then, your lawyer should tell you if it is a major problem. He should provide you with a solution. Ultimately, never buy a property until you know the title is clear. Another important point is the zoning certificates. Your attorney should check if your property is properly zoned. If the seller said there is an official unit in the basement, you need to check it. Otherwise, you may purchase a 2-unit property with an unfinished basement for the price of a 3-unit property. You need to check the purpose of your property. Either a residential or commercial zone should be used, depending on the purpose. Then your attorney should search for any local ordinance violations relating to your property. An *ordinance* is the local rules and regulations that apply to specific municipal restrictions. Ordinances can range from forbidding noise violations at night to forbidding an animal control violation and overgrown grass. Your lawyer must also verify the insurance history of the property about any possible claim that could have happened against your property in the past several years.

The most important point is to purchase a property with no legal problems. When the legal due diligence is done, your attorney issues the attorney review letter. In this letter, he will stipulate certain legal conditions as a result of his legal inspection. It is the time when you should renegotiate the deal. By now, all inspections and repair estimates must be finalised, and you have the accurate data for your calculations. So, your lawyer will include a new price in his attorney review letter. Then, it's time for the seller's attorney to react with their corrections and counterplan. You may not accept their proposals. In this case, the deal is cancelled. However, if you can find a mutual solution, your lawyer asks your permission to sign the final attorney review letter on your behalf, meaning the attorney review and inspection periods are complete and the purchase contract comes into force.

Some Useful Information About Your Legal Structure

There are many reasons you need to create a legal structure for your real estate investments: first, to be protected from any litigations. Unfortunately, it happens often in the real estate industry. Many law firms promote easy and almost free access to their services for prospects with claims associated with real estate—like mold issues, slips, and falls. They require no prepayment, ensuring they will be reimbursed by the defendant later.

The second reason is to avoid personal liability for the debts of business the real estate investors are involved in. Only a legal corporate entity is accountable for the debts and liabilities afflicted by the business—not the owners or managers.

The third purpose is to mitigate the tax burden and to avoid paying excessive taxes, especially if you are not a US resident. When you own your own corporate entity, you may deduct expenses, such as your car, telephone, cell phone, and travel, from your revenue.

There are a few ways to own US real estate through some of the most common legal entities: a Limited Liability Company (LLC), a C corporation, and a Limited Partnership (LP).

A Limited Liability Company is usually used by Americans to purchase real estate. It functions as a private limited company. This legal structure combines principles of the pass-through taxation of a sole proprietorship with the limited liability of a corporation. Foreign residents should be careful using an LLC. It depends on how their own country's legislations treat an American LLC. The tax authorities in Canada (CRA) consider an LLC as a foreign corporation (not flow through entity), resulting in a foreign tax credits discrepancy and double taxation for Canadians when they transfer their profit back to Canada. So, my advice is to avoid personal membership in an LLC when buying real estate in the United States. You can put another legal structure, like a Limited Partnership, as a sole member of an LLC. I provide an example of how a multi-entity structure might look on my book's web-site, www.MakeItBigBelowTheBorder.com, and why it could be interesting to consider. For now, I want to point out that using an LLC for your real estate investment can be a wonderful strategy if used in the right conditions. I also recommend consulting a cross-border tax specialist for their professional advice.

C Corporation. A *C corporation* is a business entity, with the same functions as a regular corporation, but the tax regulation separates its profit from the profit of owners under subchapter C of the Internal Revenue Code. The big advantage of a C corporation is the ability to reinvest profits at a lower corporate tax rate, and it is a better legal structure for real estate investors who flip properties. A C corporation allows flippers more tax breaks and deductions when running a large amount of money through a company. However, a C corporation is more expensive and tougher in maintenance than an LLC or a Limited Partnership. Once again, I want to caution you about creating a C corporation for your real estate needs if you are not a US resident. Please, apply for legal advice from knowledgeable tax professionals.

Limited Partnership (LP). A limited partnership is a business entity, with one general partner and one or more limited partners. A general partner handles all debts and liabilities of the limited partnership, while the limited partners enjoy this business structure by having legal shelter for their assets. For additional protection, another business entity, such as an LLC, is often nominated as a general partner. Sometimes, a general partner possesses only 1% of a limited partnership. Such a legal structure allows a real estate investor to gain control over an LP and minimise personal liability vulnerability. A limited partnership can be filed in any state where you want to invest, and you may use it as a holding company for LLCs, in which the LP is a sole member. You can acquire the properties directly through the series of LLC, the clones of your initial LLC, because they are less expensive in registration, they are held through a limited partnership, they provide excellent asset protection, and they will not create disadvantageous tax consequences for the foreign investor. My advice is to create a separate series LLC for each property you are acquiring. It provides you with additional protection. When it's time to sell your house, you will close this series LLC just to avoid any possible claims from future owners. There is always an insignificant risk that such claims will occur, even many years after you sold your home. Remember, a limited partnership is sole shareholder of the series LLC. From a tax point of view, an LP is also a flow-through legal entity that does not pay tax. All profits or losses come directly to the partners and are accounted for on their individual income tax returns. More information about how to structure the limited partnership efficiently is available on the book website, www.MakeItBigBelow TheBorder.com. However, for precise information, consult your attorney and tax adviser to get their expert advice. Do not be afraid to spend money for a consultation. This relatively small expense will be compensated over and above.

What Should You Do Before Closing?

About two or three weeks before closing day, you need to solve the following pending points:

- Check with your attorney to see which closing company or title agent will be chosen for closing. A title company's, or a title agent's, responsibility is to determine that a property title is clear and provide title insurance. A title company makes sure a property title is legitimate, so you, as a buyer, may be confident that, once you buy a property, you will be the rightful owner of the property. Usually, the seller's attorney proposes the title company he trusts. You need to ask your attorney what he thinks about that choice. If your lawyer feels uncomfortable with the closing company chosen by the seller's side, insist on changing it.
- Another important point is how much the closing company charges for their services. You might be surprised to find the prices of different title companies vary widely. I try not to overpay and always do my homework or consult with my attorney about how much the closing company's services will cost.
- Check again if any liens are still active on your property. If you are closing without the assistance of your attorney, ask the title company about that. Remember, one essential task of a title company is to make sure a property title is legitimate. A title company performs a title search before closing and searches for any possible issue that might affect ownership.
- Ask your attorney about a property survey for your property. It's important to survey a property before closing because it determines the boundaries of the land on which a property sits

and verifies whether there are any encroachments on the property by neighbours and any easements that may affect an ownership claim.

- Prepare a construction contract and have it signed by the general contractor who has won the bid. In chapter 8, I will tell you how to make this construction contract. I remember doing my first deal. I was not in time for preparing the construction contract. It took me one month after closing to finalise the bid, choose a winner, and sign the construction agreement with him. This resulted in significant delays in the project realisation. Learning from this experience, I try to get the construction contract signed before the closing.
- Call utility companies: electricity, gas, and water. Switch their services to your company name at closing day. I even suggest arranging pre-authorized payments because you can save time by having your bills paid regularly each month.
- Open a bank account in your company name. From that moment, all payments associated with your property will go through this bank account.
- Prepare for key transfer and lock change at closing day. Keys are not usually turned over until the closing is complete. Ask your general contractor to prepare new locks and lock box in advance.
- Ask to do a walk-through inspection before the closing. You need to coordinate this with your real estate broker. The main point is to check that the property is not vandalised and is in the same decent condition.

Don't Forget About Insurance

There is another important point you need to solve before closing. You should get proper insurance coverage. It's impossible to find a regular policy. No one insurer will issue it for you because the property will be vacant during the renovation. So, you need a different type of insurance. You need a *builder risk policy*. Remember to inform the insurance agent that, once you finish the repair work and get tenants moved in there, you will need to obtain new coverage as *landlord* to replace any builder's risk policy.

The quote of builder risk insurance should cover the structure of your property as it stands and will cover your repair improvements budget. Ask your insurer to include not less than $1,000,000 in general liability and ensure vandalism coverage is included.

My recommendation is to look for insurance a minimum of two weeks before closing. Google the list of property insurers in your target area. Ask your real estate agent and other investors for their referrals. Your goal is to find the best coverage for a good price. Remember, it takes time for an insurance broker to prepare quotes for you. Don't give up your search until you find the right insurance at an affordable price.

You also need to agree with your general contractor to put you as an additional insured in his commercial general liability insurance and to make him responsible for worker's compensation. Have the GC put your company (an LLC) as additional insured with a waiver of subrogation; this will cover you, individually, as an officer of the corporation. Waiver of subrogation is a contractual provision that bars the subcontractor's worker compensation insurer from initiating a third-party claim on you. Normally, this should be no problem for your GC to accommodate.

Closing Day: How to Organise Your Time in the Most Effective Way

On closing day, you and the seller will sign all necessary legal documents that officially transfer the title. The title agent handles verification and recording of the legal documents and collection of all necessary payments. I highly recommend delegating your attorney to represent you during the closing. There are two reasons. First, your attorney will review all closing documents before closing and can make necessary corrections straight away. Second, he can better negotiate pending issues you may discover during your final walk-through of the property, like remaining tenants or vandalised property. Try to avoid your presence during the title transfer. Provide your lawyer with power of attorney and let him close on your behalf. You have a lot of other important things to do on closing day. It would be better if you appoint a meeting with your general contractor and visit the property that day. Check that nothing on your property is vandalised, and there is no debris or personal belongings in massive quantities. Once, I had a case where I discovered the property was not cleaned out, and there was so much personal stuff in there that we needed to request a credit for dumpster service. So, I let my attorney solve the problem with the seller and renegotiate the additional credit for $4,000.

The remaining tenants who do not want to move out may also become a big problem for you. You have agreed to purchase the property without tenants because, immediately after the closing, you will make repairs. But for some unknown reason, you find the tenants are still there. They can barricade themselves in there, call the police, and request an official eviction procedure, which may take six months or more. In this situation, you have to call your attorney immediately. Usually, he knows what to do. Your attorney knows the property should be free of any liens, and any lease agreement between the seller and tenants is a lien and liability. So, he can push the seller's side to solve the problem during closing. Otherwise, the transaction can be cancelled, or he will sue them, aiming for full compensation of all your financial costs, emotional stress, and moral damage. I prefer not to be there during such tough talks, and it's an additional reason I delegate my attorney to close on my behalf and to solve all walk-through issues.

Instead, focus on the future aspect of your project that day. Walk through the building again with your contractor to work out the remaining details of repair work. Let him explain his vision of the work, so you can discuss all pending points of renovation. If you are investing from another city and have not had an opportunity to come to your first closing, you may delegate the walk-through to your general contractor. However, I recommend arriving for your first closing. You will acquire experience and feel comfortable in your following deals. Having trust and good rapport with your contractor and your attorney helps you to pass quickly through this stage in the future.

Steps to Preserving Your Property Until Repair Work

The last important point I would like to touch on in this chapter is the property preservation until you finalise financing and start repair work. It might take two or three months before you can bring a hard money loan for your first deal and start repairs. During this period, you need to preserve your property against burglary and vandalism. It could also be one of the major conditions for your property to be properly and adequately insured. So, during the walk-through with your general contractor at closing day, you need to find a solution to this issue. First, ask your general contractor to rekey the locks on all exterior doors. Ask him to install a key lock box. This must be done the same day at closing. Second, you need to install a new alarm system and/or board up all exterior doors and windows. If your property is in a high crime area, I suggest installing metallic or thick plywood guards on windows and doors throughout the property. Ask your general contractor to take care of that as soon as he can. It will cost you less than if you hire a special preservation company to install the guards.

We talked about many practical things in the last chapters. It's undoubtedly useful in real estate transactions, but you should not lose sight of the big picture. Awareness that your strategy is right will always help you out of any difficulties and unforeseen complications in the business. One important point of your strategy is a clear understanding of where you add value in your real estate deal. What should you do to increase that value, and what is your personal contribution to this process? That's what we'll talk about in more detail in the next chapter.

Chapter 7

How to Add Value

"Money flows in the direction of value."
– Author Unknown

Some people may ask why the methods in *Make It Big Below the Border* are well suited for raising property values. What distinguishes your system from your competitors? It's hard to judge because every real estate investor sticks to the technique that is more relevant to their goals, vision, and preferences. Nevertheless, my strategy includes several foundation stones, which make it an efficient tool for achieving wealth in real estate. These principles are successfully used by other investors, but here I combined them together to reach their most powerful effect. That is the advantage of *Make It Big Below the Border*. These principles will allow you to know exactly where you will gain a profit and which stages will add value. You will also be able to apply them to other strategies because they are universal in the real estate investment industry. So, let's start learning the main adding-value rules in real estate.

Focusing on Construction Improvements

The most important ground rule in your investment activity for significantly adding the value to your investment property is to focus on renovation improvements. It's one of the most obvious advantages of the *Make It Big Below the Border* strategy. When you invest without remodelling, you have limited possibilities to create a value for your property in a relatively short time. It takes a long time to build up your equity through property appreciation and paying down the mortgage principal. This approach is excellent for investing in big apartment complexes. Making repairs to your investment property means you don't have to wait long for your property equity to rise. The value of your home will rise immediately after renovation. This is quite an aggressive investment strategy. It consists foremost in finding value when you buy a distressed house below market value, and creating value when you make construction improvements that increase the selling price above their cost. As you may remember, distressed properties are initially low priced because of a lack of interest from regular buyers, and difficulties to attract conventional financing. So, you can make a significant profit by only selling your newly renovated property. However, it's easy to say, but not so easy to do. It is important to know which improvements have the potential to make a profit for you and which ones have not. Your primary task as a real estate investor is focusing on the repairs that can bring you the best result.

There are four areas you need to pay particular attention to because they are the ones that your potential clients will be most interested in:

Front look of your property, including front yard: it should have a nice view from the front and amazing landscaping. This is the first strong impression your buyers will form from your property.

Beautiful new kitchen: If the kitchen doesn't look nice, it's likely the buyer will block the decision to purchase the house.

Updated master bedroom and bathroom: they should look fresh and new. Pay attention to the master bedroom and kitchen layouts. Neither should be small and narrow.

Creating an additional unit in the basement: It works if the basement has enough ceiling height. It's a great opportunity to rent this unit out to create an additional cash flow from the rent. You just need to build a better layout in the basement with two or three bedrooms.

There is a lot more to repairing your property than just these areas. However, focusing your attention on these four premises lets you add outstanding value to your investment property in the most cost-effective way.

Focusing on Tenant Base Improvements

The second top principle of successful investments in real estate is focusing on tenant base improvements. This means you need to always seek the opportunity to improve the quality of your tenants. You can achieve this by selecting a decent location for your property and making a nice renovation. The high-end tenants permanently seek a good neighbourhood to live in, with good schools, and no crime. They also prefer a fresh, renewed house with a new kitchen and appliances, remodelled bathrooms, and enough space for their families. They feel comfortable living in such homes. That also means you have more stable long-term tenants, less vacancy, higher rents, and fewer chances of property damage. At the same time, the financial performance of your investment property is improving dramatically through increasing of NOI (Net Operating Income) and ROI (Return on Investment). The NOI and the ROI are expanding because of reduced vacancies, lower expenses for property maintenance, and increases in rents. Therefore, the value of your property is also growing.

So, the most important thing you can do after purchasing your property is to change all previous tenants and create a new image of your house as a more prestigious one. You should think creatively about how to associate your property with a tenant-friendly environment, safety, comfort, and high status. What is in your power to improve the appearance of your house and set up a relevant marketing campaign? I'm going to touch on this topic more in detail in chapter 9, which is dedicated to property management. For now, it's enough that you understand the basics of this principle.

Increasing Your Equity

The third top element on my list is equity build-up. It doesn't need your personal involvement as in the previous two cases. It runs in parallel with the very nature of the real estate market and by the financial structure of the real estate transaction. That is to say, the equity grows in two directions. Here is how it works:

The first part of the equity accumulation comes through property appreciation. Appreciation is an increase in the value of an asset over time. Real estate is an asset that unavoidably grows in value in the long term. Certainly, there could be long periods of recession and stagnation in any real estate market. In some emerging markets, real estate investors wait a long time for sustainable real estate growth. Nevertheless, real estate always expands in value in the long term, and it happens very slowly. However, its power has the same effect as the compound interest in finance and can create enormous wealth for you if you have enough patience and do it the right way.

The second part comes through your tenants paying off your mortgage principal. Are you aware that tenants pay all your expenses on the property, including your mortgage? Nevertheless, it is so. Your goal as a real estate investor is to choose the right deal in which you still have something left in your pocket. All in all, your tenants are working hard to earn money, some portion of which goes to purchasing the property for you. It's quite possible that the same happens while you are shopping—part of your money that paid for the product you like goes towards the mortgage reimbursement of that commercial property. So, that's how the economy works and develops today.

I'm going to illustrate how these two components can bring success to any intelligent investments in real estate. In this example, I'm omitting the construction work and assuming you have bought a property in good condition. Let's suppose you have bought a two-unit property for $300,000. The bank is ready to provide you with a mortgage for 80% of the purchase price, i.e. $240,000. The bank can credit your house at 5% for a period of 25 years. Your monthly payment to the bank would be $1,395.85. (I used an online mortgage payment calculator to get this information.) Besides the interest payment to the bank, it repays the portion of your loan—the mortgage principal. After five years, your debt to the bank would be $212,425 and after 10 years it will drop to $177,126.

Let's assume that during the first two years, the real estate in your area grows by 2% each year, and by 4% over the next three years. Thus, your property will rise in price up to $351,000 in five years. We may also assume that in the next following five years, its value will increase to $420,000.

Therefore, if you decide to sell your house in five years, you will have $138,575 after debt payment to the bank. After subtracting the amount of your down payment, your net profit will be $78,575 for five years, and your annual ROI (Return on Investment) will achieve 26%! Not so bad. If you want to sell your house in 10 years, your net income would be $182,874 for ten years or 30% in ROI. It's still a decent profit. This is how it works in real estate. In the long run, you are going to get a significant profit! The sooner you start investing, the greater the return on your investment.

Rent Cash Flow is King

So, cash flow is the king. It's the fourth foundation stone of my strategy. You should never, ever buy a property that loses money each month. Don't buy a property with negative cash flow! You should check it even before putting in your offer. Do you remember the formula I provided you with in chapter 4, for how to calculate the net operating income? Yes, the NOI is the Gross Collected Rents minus the Vacancy Rate and all the Expenses on the property. Now, I'm going to introduce you to another formula which will help you with the idea of whether or not your property can bring you positive cash flow after renovation. However, you won't need this formula if you don't want to use a mortgage to finance your property. In this case, the positive cash flow you get from rentals is the net operating income of your property. Nevertheless, this new formula would be useful if you want a mortgage to finance your house. That's why investors use the terms of the conventional financing specific for area and property they want to invest in, as well as the online mortgage payment calculator. They need all that information just to know how much their mortgage payment to the bank is. At first sight, it might seem complicated, but I assure you that after doing it a couple of times, you will find it easy. Here is the formula:

Debt Coverage Ratio (DCR) = Net Operating Income (NOI) / Debt Service

Debt Coverage Ratio is a measure of the cash flow available to pay current debt obligations, and debt service is your mortgage payments to the bank. If the net operating income of your property is less than the mortgage payment, it means your property is generating a negative cash flow and you will lose money each month. If NOI is more than the mortgage payment, your property brings you a positive cash flow each month. There is one nuance—the bank also uses this formula to check whether they want to give you a mortgage or not. Usually, they want a debt coverage ratio of more than 1.3. That's great for you too! You know in advance if the bank is going to give you the mortgage in each particular case. Let's assume that NOI for a certain project is $66,000 and the annual mortgage payments are $47,000. After dividing one figure by the other, we get a DCR of 1.4. That's enough to be confident that the bank will give you a mortgage. Using the debt coverage ratio formula could be helpful to check whether certain areas or types of property are capable of generating a positive cash flow. If you live in an area where a positive cash flow is impossible, you need to find another area to invest in. If you find that investing in single-family houses in your neighbourhood is not profitable, purchasing a multi-family dwelling can be an excellent way to go. That's the reason why we recommend your investing in two, three, and four- unit properties in *Make It Big Below the Border.*

Adding Value For Your Investor. The Magic of Refinancing

Now we come closer to the most interesting concept, which will allow you to return the money invested in the project. I'm talking about refinancing. Let's start with an example in which I assume that you are purchasing a two-unit property for $110,000 in a certain area. Then you need to repair it for $65,000. Your property value, after repairs, will be $285,000. In three months, you have a plan to put great tenants in your property. It takes another two months to select the best inhabitants. After one year of stabilising your property, after everything goes smoothly with the rents, you can apply for refinancing to one of the smaller local banks in your area. You will ask for regular mortgage refinancing at a low-interest rate and a long amortisation period. After considering your case, the bank may take the decision to finance your house at 80% of the current market value, i.e. $228,000. So, you are going to receive this money as cash. Aside from the amount of $175,000 that covers your purchase and repair costs, you will get $53,000 in net profit!

By implementing refinancing, you get the same desirable result as selling your house—you receive cash. You will reimburse all your investments in the project! If you attract a hard money loan to finance the repair work, you can repay that loan first and reinvest the rest in another project! So, thanks to this financial tool, you can now act like a real estate deal machine, creating multiple projects!

Don't forget that your property remains yours, and you continue to get a positive cash flow every single month. Your new mortgage liability is paid by your tenants, not by you, as well as other expenses related to your property.

Furthermore, after refinancing, your deal has the great potential for attracting investors. I repeat: refinancing creates an opportunity for the benefit of your potential investor. It is true. First, he is going to invest in a safe asset, which is your property. Then, he gets his money back at refinancing and still stays in the deal, receiving his part of the rental cash flow.

It is also a great opportunity for you to scale your real estate business and to MAKE IT really BIG! So, when starting each new great project, you don't need to mobilise your own money; you can bring in money from other people!

Important Points to Know About Refinancing

There are a few points you should be aware of regarding refinancing. Your goal is to negotiate suitable and advantageous conditions for you with the bank. A few months in advance, create a list of local banks in your area. Then, send them a message with a brief description of your property. Tell them that you are still stabilising your property and that you have just rented it out to new tenants several months before. You will receive feedback from a few of those banks and they will provide you with their conditions. You need to select the banks that are ready to issue a regular mortgage at 80% after repair value. Regular terms of their refinancing mortgage mean standard interest rates and a long-term amortisation period. The stabilising time may vary between six and twelve months. Keep in mind you should show the bank that your property is rented to good, reliable, and long-term tenants.

A hard money lender who provided you with the construction loan may also propose that you refinance your property. However, I don't find their conditions advantageous. Usually, they can refinance for the same amount they have already given to you as a hard money loan, i.e. not more than 65% of the purchase price and repair costs.

The final, most important, point about refinancing is that you don't need to pay taxes on it. When you get money from refinancing, it is tax-free, as this is technically not a profit. You just receive a new liability—a new loan from the bank. So, you have an incredible opportunity to save on taxes while reinvesting that money in your next great projects. Your goal is not to spend all that money and waste, but to reinvest in your next real estate project. This is the route to your wealth in real estate.

Now you have a complete picture of how to add value. As you may have noticed, the content of this book is based on a clear narration of the benefits and profits you will get by applying my methods. The rest of my book is a set of practical recommendations to follow my blueprint and avoid costly mistakes. It's time to learn about many interesting and useful things in the organisation and management of repair work. This is a crucial stage when investors either lose their money by doing things the wrong way or make money if they follow the proven system. We will talk about these issues in the next chapter.

Chapter 8

How to Manage Repairs

"Create with the heart; build with the mind."
– Criss Jami

Repairing the property can be the most challenging part of your whole real estate investment journey. It is where you will spend a lot of your money, so you need to learn how to skillfully control such spending and keep your profit. Seasoned real estate investors make money when they buy. So, they should also keep their money when they repair. They can do it by ably controlling their general contractors, who control the repairs. So, you should learn to act in the same way. In this chapter, we will focus on how to control contractors and manage your renovation in an efficient manner.

Final Bid: Get as Much Information From Each Contractor and Choose the Best One

The first step toward your control over repairs is the selection of the best general contractor for your project. The rule is simple: the more initial work you do to find and to add more good contractors to your list, the better your choice among the worthy candidates and the more chances you will pre-qualify the right professional. Don't hesitate to ask them to show you current and recently finished projects and referrals. Call their clients and talk to them about their experience working with that particular GC. Visit all their construction sites to look at their team, their quality of work, and quality of finish. Ask them about prices for each kind of work you are interested in. So, there is a lot of work you need to do even before the closing. You establish your control over repairs then. For your first project, you may not hold a bid before the closing date but, next time, you will learn how to organise it on schedule. You will save a lot of time, and time is paramount in this business.

During the bid, as you are going through the building and listening carefully to the contractors you invited to bid, you will learn a lot about your property, as well as the specifics of doing business in your city. Also, you can compare their different approaches. Just try to listen carefully to all their proposals. If you are not in the city, contact all your bidders by Skype, or by phone, and discuss each item related to repairs, step by step.

My advice is not to choose the contractor who will offer the lowest price. Choose the one who will provide the most efficient and creative solutions, will provide good quality, and will do all the work on time. Choose the one who craves this work—the one with a fire in his eyes, perseverance, and determination to do the work for you—intuition should tell you.

Once you have made your choice, you need to do paperwork. You need to collect the most recent copies of his general contractor licence and W9 tax form. The W9 form provides the taxpayer identification number and certification information about a general contractor and is needed when investors file their tax returns to write off all payments made to their contractors. As I mentioned in chapter 6, ask your general contractor to include your company as an additional insured with a waiver of subrogation in his general liability and worker compensation insurance. Then you should sign a contract with him.

Important Points to Put in Your Contractor Agreement

The contract with your general contractor is the most important part of managing your repair work. It has the same gravity as establishing good business relations with him and performing your obligations, such as on-time payments and the opportunity to work on your next project, if you are satisfied with his current work.

I provide you with a free contract sample on www.MakeItBig BelowtheBorder.com that you can download and review. However, I think it would be good if you know the key points of the contract you need to pay attention to. Then, ask your lawyer to prepare a contract for you, considering all these elements I mention in the book.

Over time, there might be significant changes in the legislation, which can affect many provisions in the contract. It's hard to predict. Besides, the legislation may vary from state to state. Therefore, to draw up the right contract, my advice is to apply for the assistance of your attorney. Do not skimp on it because a composed sample of your construction contract will serve you repeatedly in all your projects.

First, pay attention to the *name of the contract.* I advise to call it *Independent Contractor Agreement,* confirming an independent status of your general contractor.

Basic information about your contractor. Your GC should provide his name and address, his company name and address, his cell phone number, phone number at home (obligatory), his GC's licence and registration number, and contractor's tax identification number.

Permits and licences. It should be clearly stipulated that your general contractor pulls all necessary permits and licences needed for construction work. If you need architectural drawings, ask your contractor and real estate agent to refer you to a good architect, who can do the job relatively inexpensively. Indicate in the contract the cost and timing of architectural work and the need for well-coordinated interaction between the contractor and the architect when implementing the drawings.

Indemnifications article should impose a general contractor to compensate, and hold you harmless, as a client, from any worker compensation claims and liabilities, and claims imposed by governmental bodies and courts relating to the contractor and his employees.

Insurance. Indicate in the contract which kind of insurance your GC must provide.

Independent contractor status should confirm your general contractor and his team are not your employees. You need it to avoid potential tax and liability issues. You may underline you are responsible neither for employment nor any training of the people in your GC's crew. You are also not responsible for procuring them with the tools and equipment.

Materials. Here, you should explain how your contractor is responsible for the procurement of materials. Get rid of the temptation to buy materials yourself. First, you can be physically doing business from another city. Second, you avoid the mess when your general contractor calls you each day asking to coordinate the purchase of missing materials, their price, and specifications.

Work supervision article preserves your right to inspect the property, to stop work, and to prescribe alterations for the purpose to check the quality and conformity of work with that specified in the agreement. You may hire another person or company to be your representative on this issue.

Extra work. This clause obliges to coordinate all changes and modifications in the contract by written agreement between the parties. Any unplanned, additional work performed by the contractor must also be agreed with by you in writing. The contractor does not have the right to increase the cost of work specified in the contract. Otherwise, he risks paying the difference out of his pocket.

Deadline penalties. This provision must stipulate you will deduct a penalty for any significant backlog in work accomplishments from any payments to the contractor. Fix penalties for each calendar day.

Right to work in the US for GC's crew. Your general contractor's personnel should be legally authorised to work in the United States under immigration legislation.

Communications clause designates you and your GC agree to timely and promptly respond to any message from the other party. It is vital for rapid and successful completion of the work.

Scope of Work and Draw Schedule are Important Parts of Your Contractor Agreement

The scope of work and the payment (draw) schedule are important documents in addition to the construction contract. After getting the work estimates from all your bidders, you should thoroughly work them out and create your own scope of work. As I said in chapter 5, you need to insist on the detailed description of each repair, with its cost for each room in your house. In reality, this is not so easy to achieve, since contractors are busy people, and the maximum they want to do is to provide their prices on each type of work for the whole project, not for each room. However, you should insist that they submit their quotes per your requirements.

There is another nuance when you face a temptation to make the finishes more perfect and luxurious than necessary, or conversely, to save on some particular types of work. This can lead to undesirable consequences. When pulling out all comparatives from your real estate agents, try to observe through the pictures the quality of finishes in all sold properties, in the same price range in which you want to sell your house. This is precisely the quality of finishes you must provide your customers. Not better and not worse. If you over-renovate, then there will be cost overruns, and repairs will pour out a pretty penny, so the project will become unprofitable. Even with nice luxury upgrades, you cannot sell the property for the price higher than ARV in your sector. If you under-renovate, it will be difficult to sell the house to future buyers or to lease to decent tenants. Therefore, try to adhere strictly to the selected quality level.

So, you include a detailed description of the work in your independent contractor agreement in your scope of work. The more accurate and thorough it will be, the better for you. This should be a very precise illustration with the prices for each type of work and for each room, kitchen, and bathroom in your property. You may divide it into the exterior and interior work. Specify that all tools, equipment, installation, and finishing materials for the project, such as paint, sheetrock, patching, and framing materials, must be provided by your contractor. He must acquire all that at his own expense.

You need to determine the terms of your scope of work, i.e., the date when the project starts and the expected date of its completion. Once again, don't forget to mention the penalty for expired days.

Also, designate the amount of compensation to your contractor, i.e., the cost of all planned work and the scheme of payments. It's better to place this payout timeline in a separate document, called the *Draw Schedule*. Talk about this important legal paper with your contractor. It is important to know the sequence of work implementations. Distribute all work in three or four tranches. You should determine the cost of work and the cost of material for each draw and incorporate them in the contractor agreement. Since you take a construction loan from a hard money lender, all payments will be made after performing all designated work in each draw. These are the rules of a hard money loan! Although you can provide your GC with a prepayment for demolition works, just to show him your goodwill, I recommend not exceeding it for over two or three thousand dollars. Clarify that you have no other money for repairs than the borrowed money. Provide your contractor with a confirmation letter from your lender that the construction loan is approved and ready for use. He must be sure he will be paid for his work and materials because he has to accumulate sufficient funds to pay his team and for the materials in advance.

Material and Labor Lead Time

During preparation of the scope of work, you need to consider that some materials require certain time necessary for their manufacturing. Otherwise, it will delay your project timeline. You need to take care of that and order these materials in advance, long before their installation is scheduled. This applies especially to the lead time of windows and doors, kitchen cabinets and some types of expensive tiles, metal bars on windows and doors, etc. Pay particular attention to the windows. Such a seemingly unimportant detail can slow down the repairs of your property. Delays can be calculated in weeks.

A similar situation can happen with your construction people. Sometimes your general contractor might invite some rare professionals from outside, who may not always be available. It may cause delays. However, this is beyond your competence; let your contractor solve this problem. Your business is just to push your contractor to try to avoid such situations. Another point is when your contractor is busy with other projects and cannot immediately start working on your property. This point is the subject to agree in your Contractor Agreement. You need the precise date of commencement of construction in the scope of work part of your contract.

Pulling out the permits for certain types of work and preparation of architectural drawings may cause severe delays at the beginning of the project. Ask your contractor to take care of getting the permits immediately and to begin demolition and other work not in need of permits at the same time.

Three Important Keys to Help You Stay Organised: Quality, Timing, Budget

You need to learn how to manage three critical components of your repairs: quality, time, and costs.

The *quality* of finishing and other types of work must be negotiated and agreed with the contractor in advance and fixed in the scope of work's amendment of the contract. There are also special clauses in the contract allowing you to control and supervise the quality of work. You have the right to hire another person or a company to act as your representative and to monitor the progression of the work. You have the right to stop or interrupt construction if something is wrong, either with the quality or conformity with the essential clauses of the contract. In reality, you should insist on the contractor sending you pictures of the work progress each week. It really helps.

However, you should choose the quality of all finishing materials yourself, especially the kitchen cabinets, countertops, and appliances. Ask where your GC buys the kitchen cabinets for his clients. Try also to find other suppliers. Go there. Ask for estimates, compare the prices, and choose the kitchen you like for your property. Similarly, you need to choose tiles for your bathroom, kitchen floor, and backsplash. Typically, you don't need much ceramics for performing one bathroom and one kitchen, so it's better to buy the expensive but nicer tiles. You will not save much, but the look of your bathroom and kitchen backsplash will be much more attractive. Try to make everything look new and fresh. Paint colour, trims, hardwood floor, bathroom, kitchen, appliances, fixtures, etc. — everything should look new. Do not leave old materials. They will look even more awful next to the new ones. Don't put new kitchen appliances with upgraded but old kitchen cabinets.

Time. Each month of repair work costs you at least a monthly interest payment to your hard money lender. Each month of delay would cost you significantly more. So, timing is highly critical. At the stage of drafting and signing the contract, talk to the contractor about the schedule of work implementation. Divide this job timeline by draws and by months. Then, control this work schedule thoroughly. Call your general contractor twice a week. Ask him about work progress and about delays, if any. Ask him about the reasons for each backlog. At the end of each week, request pictures. Your contractor is also interested in completing work on each draw as soon as possible and in getting faster payment. Your task is to aim him at the timely execution of each step.

Cost control. The cost of work, the budget, and the payment procedure must be agreed in advance in the contractor agreement. There may be surprises during construction; no one is immune. Your contractor may find rotten floor that must be changed under the tile in the bathroom. It can be a damaged sewer pipe under the building. It's difficult to predict such situations in advance. You must be psychologically ready for a sudden increase in the cost. My advice is to foresee an additional 10% provision in your total budget for such bad surprises.

However, it is necessary for your contractor to know that all the increases in the budget will be difficult to coordinate, not only with you, but also with your lender. He has an approved draw schedule, under which money is allocated. Before each draw payment, the lender sends his inspector to check compliance of performed work to the scope of work in the contract. If something is wrong, the general contractor has a risk of not getting his money, or getting it when all discrepancies are eliminated. In addition, he must realise you do not have other money to pay for his services. This helps keep your contractor within the budget.

Closing Out the Construction

Upon completion of repair work, you have to perform certain paper procedures. Before you send the last draw's payment to your contractor, which should be not less than 10% of the entire project cost, you need to resolve issues for two legal papers. I would like to underline that both documents are an integral part of the Independent Contractor Agreement incorporated as additional amendments.

The first document is a *Contractor Punch Out List*. This final punch list specifies the remaining deficiencies, after the repairs, which you want the contractor to eliminate before receiving the last payment. It should be signed by both parties. The contractor agrees all the points specified in the punch list will be eliminated before your final inspection. When all is done, you sign off on this list that all issues are fixed.

The second paper is a *Final Waiver of Lien*, in which the contractor confirms he has received all the payment due to him and he has no problems with you. He ensures in writing that he waives any claim on any possible lien against you or your property, and he won't file a complaint in the future. You will sign this waiver of lien after all issues related to the final punch list are solved. So, the project is considered finished, and you should pay him the balance when the waiver of lien is signed.

Actually, if you need to obtain the renovation permits, you may need one more document to be arranged. You must get the certificate of occupancy signed by the city authorities. They confirm in writing that your permissions cease to be valid due to the completion of repair work. However, you need no certificate of occupancy if you make a cosmetic renovation in your property and need no building permit.

Preparing Property for Section 8 Inspection

After the repair, you have two options: either sell your house for a higher price or rent it out to the right tenants. The strategy of this book implies the second approach. It appears here an excellent opportunity to raise your project and your investments to a safer and more sustainable level. I'm talking about the possibility to rent your property to the tenants supported by the federal government's Housing Choice Voucher Program, widely known as the *Section 8*. It got this name because of the paragraph number in the Federal housing act of 1937, which establishes this program. The Section 8 program pays a significant part of the rent for families with insufficient income. They receive a housing voucher, which covers most of the rent payment. The government considers the coverage amount in each case. This is a unique opportunity for investors because it provides the stability of rent payments. Regular tenants might lose their jobs or have huge, unexpected medical expenses not covered by an adequate insurance policy. Such situations significantly affect the delay in rent payments. With Section 8, you are always sure you will receive a monthly cheque from the government to pay for your Section 8 tenants.

There are other advantages of the Section 8 program for investors. Under this Section 8 program, there are many restrictions for voucher holders. With various violations, the housing voucher can be easily lost. If a tenant does not pay his portion of the rent, then he will lose his voucher. If a tenant deteriorates your property, you can sue him, and he loses his voucher. You can rely on government compensation for damages caused by your Section 8 tenant. If a tenant behaves badly and you often receive complaints from other tenants, or the police are a frequent guest at your property, then after several warnings, he can lose his voucher. There is no hassle with rent collection; money comes automatically with no delay to your account. If you continue to prequalify the best tenants among candidates with a voucher, they will be the better choice than regular tenants. My advice is always to select among the tenants eligible for Section 8 program. To apply for the program, you need to fill out the relevant legal papers. Let your property manager take care of that. In chapter 3, you learned how to find this professional. He can be helpful for you in another important case: preparing your property for Section 8 inspection. It also falls within his competence. You should also know enough about this subject because its preparation starts at the repair phase of your project.

Preparing for Section 8 inspection. Check that everything in your house is properly prepared. Everything must be clean, tidy, in good condition, not broken, and functioning perfectly. This is easy to achieve because you just finished repairs. It is likely the first inspection will fail. You should not be upset because almost all landlords face such a situation. It is necessary to understand that the inspector who comes with an inspection is a real professional. He ensures the tenants covered by this government program have the opportunity to live only in good, safe, clean dwellings, and only caring and merited landlords must get government money. So, it seems to be a hard procedure. The objections can touch everything—exposed electrical wiring, not in service utilities, not working smoke and carbon monoxide detectors, electrical outlets and light fixtures, etc. Take the matter seriously and, with the assistance of your contractor, eliminate all the shortcomings. You must be ready for Section 8 inspection from the moment of your repairs. That's why the final punch-out list is essential. It helps you to get your property clean, safe, and functional toward the inspection. Insist on your contractor paying attention to it. Then it would be easier for you to pass through this inspection.

You have already noticed, as in many previous stages, it will be difficult to succeed without the help of a real professional. It's the same when you rent your property. You need somebody trustworthy and efficient to find suitable and reliable tenants, to pass through Section 8 inspection, and to manage your property while you are investing from another city, or even from another country. You need a great property manager for your house. Know about requirements his work must meet and how to focus him on efficient work so your property earns you a stable income. Now it's time to learn how to manage your property manager. We will discuss that at large in the next chapter.

Chapter 9

How to Manage a Property Manager

"Quality means doing it right when no one is looking."
– Henri Ford

From now on, starting a new chapter, I will insist you take active steps. Improvements in any business come with practice, and not only with theoretical knowledge. I hope that by now you have already selected the city in which you will invest, and have also created your real estate team. Do not wait, but start acting. Now, we begin the crucial topic of renting out your property and managing your tenants.

Once the builders have finished making repairs, you will need a good property management company for the sustainable administration of your house and to provide quality services to your tenants. Earlier in the chapter, which was devoted to the creation of your team, we talked about why you need and how to find this professional. I cannot imagine managing your property without someone's skilled help if you invest from Canada or some other country. There must always be someone in the same city as your house who will take care of it and the tenants. So, the key position in such a responsible job is assigned to a property manager. This person, or his company, will help your property to generate a positive cash flow regularly. He and his strong crew have all necessary skills to run your house and to serve your tenants in the most efficient way. As soon as you learn how to manage the property manager, you can delegate all of the menial tasks to them, free your time, and expand and scale your real estate business. Those professionals are here so you can buy more houses that generate profit, and reinvest it to buy more profitable properties again. This will build your real estate empire. In this chapter, we will focus on everything you must learn about making a property manager one of the most productive and loyal members of your team.

How to Prequalify the Right Property Management Company

Earlier, in chapter 3, we talked about where and how to find them. I recommended you make a list of ten names, and meet with the first three people during your first visit to the city and visual inspection of your property. Now, it's time to talk about criteria by which you should select good property managers. Keep in mind to prepare questions to ask them during the first meeting.

First, how long have they been in the business? I advise you to select the companies with over ten years of experience in this field.

How many buildings in total have they got under their management? It is important they can supervise many properties together and have an extensive customer base. Managing multiple buildings simultaneously might mean their business is sustainable, and their clients are satisfied with the services. They should have enough time and resources to manage your house. Otherwise, it could be another problem.

Do they manage other real estates in your area, near your property? They must be present in your neighbourhood. If yes, ask for addresses, and then check these properties online. There must be the company's signboard attached to the front wall of the buildings. I even advise you to walk over and talk to the tenants. Just ask them whether they are happy with their property manager. For sure, you will gather much useful information. If your manager does not work in your sector, this is a serious reason to look for another candidate.

Do they have enough experience in managing 2–4 unit properties? It is undesirable for you if they only specialize in multi-apartment complexes and commercial real estate. Ask how many two-unit houses they have in their portfolio at the moment. If they manage only one or two, and the rest of their selection are huge apartment buildings, it's a reason to rethink your decision about choosing this company.

In which local and national property management associations do they participate? They could be the active members of the Institute of Real Estate Managers (IREM) and the National Association of Residential Property Managers (NARPM). Participation in these associations adds credibility to your property manager. You may also check online the list of members of each association presently working for the property management company you would like to hire.

Another question is whether their clients sued them in the past. If yes, let them explain the circumstances. Inquire what the reason was and how the dispute was resolved.

You also should know how much they ask for their services. What is the monthly payment and which services does it cover? Are there separate payments from this? Do they charge an extra fee for the marketing of your property, tenant screening, and eviction services? Do they require any advance payment upon signing the contract with you?

Ask whether they can provide you with a brochure describing their services, and their policies on various topics, such as retaining good tenants, avoiding discrimination issues, and property maintenance.

You should ask all these general questions, related to your property manager, at your first meeting. Further, I will touch on many other aspects of real estate management, including the requirements your property manager must meet. For a print-ready list of these questions, and more to keep handy when interviewing your potential property manager, go to www.MakeItBigBelowTheBorder.com.

Control Your Property Manager, Not Your Tenants

My strategy focuses on resolving all issues only related to tenants helped by your property manager. Here, I do not provide information on how to work directly with tenants. I believe you should not have direct contact with them. Let your property manager deal with tenants. Just learn the duties and responsibilities of your property manager; it helps a lot to control their work. Here are some useful tips on how you can exercise such control over them.

First, you must know by which parameters to evaluate their work. The best way to do so is by using the financial indicators of your property. They reveal the true status of your project—whether your home turns into a reliable asset or loses money and becomes a liability. A clear understanding of how to increase revenue and reduce costs will assist you in adequately assessing the performance of your property manager in the future.

Seasoned real estate investors are watching to ensure that NOI of their properties (Net Operating Income) constantly remains at a high level. They work hard to increase it, and in no way allow it to decline. The NOI is important because its growth increases the cost of the building. Also, it MAKES the cash flow, coming in your pocket, BIG. As you already know from previous chapters, the NOI comprises gross operating income minus vacancies and all associated expenses. You can monitor the situation by strengthening the gross operating income. It is possible to increase rent each year and employ other sources of income, such as the coin-operated washer and dryer and the additional fees for garage/parking lot use. Determine which work a property manager must do for this. You can also influence the situation by reducing the vacancies in your property.

You should monitor how effectively the property manager can fill the vacated apartment by new tenants, how he will perform marketing your property, and how diligently he selects new tenants to minimise the downtime of vacant premises. Finally, you must control your investment through expenses reduction. Define the amount of monthly property management fees and the services you need to pay extra. Ask about their measures to control all the costs related to maintenance, current repairs, and contractual services, like snow removal or grass mowing. Also, inquire what they do to avoid additional costs. All mentioned financial indicators of your property allow you to assess how well your property management company works. Don't forget you are now not only in the real estate business; you are in the business of interacting with people and providing them with your services. Because you do not contact the tenants directly, the interaction between them and the property manager has high significance. Determine from the beginning and control the level of their communication. It must always reach high standards. Your tenants should feel great about living in your property. Also, avoid any discrimination issues during tenants' selection, rent collection, and resolving disputes between tenants.

The most important tool in governing your property manager is the property management contract you must sign with him. This agreement legally fixes the rights and obligations of both parties in managing your property. Be careful when signing it because your property manager always has a draft of the agreement at hand, and many crucial points could be accidentally, or deliberately, omitted, which might become a bad surprise for you later.

Just as you would not rent a property without a signed lease agreement that specifies the rights and responsibilities of you and your tenants, never hire a management company without having the rights and responsibilities spelled out for you and the company. Any assumptions can lead to significant losses, so it's worth negotiating all issues from the very beginning. Here, I indicate the important points you should always include in your contract.

Independent contractor status. The contract must require an independent status for your property manager. He and his crew should not be your employees. Otherwise, you may lose the tax protection provided by this *independent contractor/customer* relationship. Define from the beginning the terms of reference of your property manager and give him the freedom to act within the frame of this agreement. Know that excessive control could also lead to the loss of contractor status.

Employees of your property manager. Independent contractor status allows your manager to hire employees to perform all necessary work in your property. It's the responsibility of your property manager to pay their salaries, wages, and other compensations. The manager commits to apply his diligent efforts to hire and supervise all necessary personnel for operating your house. You, as a customer, have no right to supervise or manage his people, but you can require reassignment or dismissal of any of them.

Property management fees. This is one of the most important parts of the contract, allowing you to avoid unnecessary costs. Look carefully at the list of services covered by the monthly management fee. Often, this list doesn't comprise some of the most vital functions. Property managers want them to be paid separately. Don't accept that. The services, covered by monthly management fees, should include rent collections, bill payment, money transfers to you, accounting and bookkeeping, marketing and advertising of vacant units, tenant screening, proper communication with tenants, regular property inspection, property maintenance, trips to sudden emergency calls, adequate communication with you, etc. Find out which services you need to pay as extra fees and how much. They could be repair work, unit preparation for new tenants, filling vacant units with new tenants, eviction of bad tenants, or resolving unforeseen technical problems such as a pipe leaking. Make sure these services are listed in the agreement, so you can avoid trouble later.

Obtaining the proper insurance. The management agreement specifies the types of insurance and the amount of coverage they require. The property manager maintains, at his own expense, the public liability insurance in an amount not less than three million dollars. Ask him about other policies required by law and needed to protect both owner and manager, including worker compensation insurance, professional liability, employee practices, and fidelity insurance. In the case of any accidents and damage relating to the property operation and maintenance, the manager should investigate and report to the insurance company. Such a report will be timely filed and include the estimated cost of repairs. The policy must cover liability or expenses to the injured person or damage to property, resulting from the negligence of the manager or their employees and independent contractors.

Manager's Standard of Care. Direct your manager to perform duties in a manner compliant with professional property management ethics and services. The quality of his services should not be worse than those professionally carried out by other property managers in the same neighborhood. You should benefit from the experience and expertise of all members of his team involved in the operation of your property. If they have a company code of ethics, they should manage your property regarding its policies.

Fair housing regulation. Fair Housing laws protect customers (tenants and buyers) against illegal discrimination regarding: race, color, religion, sex, national origin, disability, or familial status. Such situations happen when someone is refused to rent or to buy a house due to the abovementioned reasons. Also, it may happen when property managers set different terms, conditions, or privileges for the sale or rental of a property, or provide different housing services or facilities, or make housing unavailable for discriminative purposes. The maximum penalties for violating the Fair Housing laws are $16,000. Besides, there are attorney fees and costs. It's painful and expensive, so instruct your property manager to treat everyone equally and avoid violating any of the protections under the Fair Housing laws. It's the US Department of Housing and Urban Development (HUD) who enforces the Fair Housing regulations and investigates complaints.

Control Your Finances and Organize Your Filing System

To invest in real estate successfully, you need to know your numbers and build a system to monitor your financial flows. To do this, you must coordinate with your property manager on financial statements and accounting.

Accounting, Financial Reporting, Record Keeping. First, the responsibility of the property manager for accounting and financial reporting must be reflected in the contract, where he agrees to do it well and accurately. Every state has varying legislation regarding the accounting procedures for property management. Therefore, his activity must comply with these laws. Also, the American tax authorities, the IRS, requires accurate reporting of the income and expenses on your property. Ensure interaction between your accountant and property manager, so financial reporting and accounting are conducted correctly and on time.

Check that the manager provides monthly, quarterly, and annual reports with the statement of cash flow. A skilled manager is usually well organized with all pertinent records, reports, and appropriate computer programs for their business. Ask whether he has modern and updated software allowing him to do that. Also, the property manager should have separate books, journals, and orderly files, containing rental records, insurance policies, leases, correspondence, receipts, bills, Section 8 vouchers, and all other documents pertaining to the operations of the property. You, as the owner, may inspect any records at any reasonable time upon prior notice.

Bank account. The next important point is the opening of the operating account into which the property manager will deposit and accumulate all rent and other funds collected from the property's operation. Approve the bank where the operating account is opened. The bank will be informed by your manager in writing that the funds are held in trust for the owner. You need to be on the signature cards of your account with the manager. Out of this operating account, the manager will pay the operating expenses and any other payments pertaining to the property, within the terms of the property management agreement. If the operating account contains insufficient funds to meet current expenses and a reasonable reserve, you, as an owner, will provide them before the commencement of rental income from the property. You and your property manager should set up adequate reserves needed for the normal operation of your house.

Only the sum of money exceeding reserves will be transferred directly to your personal account. The reserves should not be placed in the general account. They could be put into another interest-bearing account until needed, but always under your control. Be careful of possible complications when the operation and reserve accumulation accounts are not separate from any other accounts of your manager. Also, be vigilant and try to avoid the situation where the bank is also a creditor of your manager for his other projects.

Security Deposits. Coordinate with your manager the security deposit collected up-front from all new tenants. Then, it will be specified and reflected in the tenant's lease. Your manager maintains detailed records of all security deposits, and you have the right to inspect them anytime. The manager needs your approval to return a security deposit for the amount that exceeds $1000 to any tenant.

Rent collection. The key thing to remember is that the main source of your profit is coming from the rent. If that money is not available for your use, the project loses all meaning. So, the manager will endeavor to collect all rent and other possible charges due from tenants, such as parking income, tenant storage, and coin-operated vending machines. The property manager must systematically collect the rent and ensure tenants pay on time. It requires consistency and discipline. Insist tenants pay rent on the first day of each month with no excuse. If the manager accepts delays for some tenants, be sure other inhabitants have the right to the same privilege. Otherwise, there is a risk of the fair housing violation, resulting in a very severe penalty. On the 10th of each month, the property manager must send all that's left on the operating account to your personal account. Also, insist that employees of the management company, handling money, are bonded and insured. It provides better protection and responsibility during rent collection. When some tenants do not pay on time, the property manager should sue them or take legal action with your prior approval.

Control Your Maintenance and Repairs

The property manager should apply diligent efforts to maintain the property in good condition, including painting and carpentry, interior and exterior cleaning, plumbing, and other standard maintenance and minor repairs as may be necessary or reasonably desirable. Such maintenance and minor repairs should be coordinated with you and allocated in advance. Be careful of a *hold-harmless* provision in the agreement, stipulating your property manager is not responsible for the quality of services provided by other service or renovation companies. Ask your lawyer to find a reasonable solution. You can also force your manager to employ a rational caution when they hire a contractor to repair your property.

Also, stipulate in the contract, the manager can not incur any individual item of repair or replacement over two hundred dollars without your written authorization. With emergency repairs for the preservation and safety of the property or danger of injury to people, all essential work may be done by the manager without your approval. The property manager cannot perform maintenance and repair in a way that violates any laws, regulations, and restrictions applicable to the property or that expose you, as an owner, to the risk of liability to tenants or other people.

Contract services. Your property manager should have no right to enter any contract service agreements without your prior approval. The contract services are paid at the owner's expenses, so, they should be assigned in the owner's name or define the property manager as an owner's agent. Some contracts for recurring services could be in the manager's name since they do not involve large sums of money. Remember, the contracts with extended duration or above a certain amount of money could be subject to competitive bid. Your manager will also require that adequate insurance covers all contractors.

Problems with the Property Manager and How to Solve Them

Sometimes things go wrong with a property manager. It often happens with beginner investors who have not diligently chosen the right professional. They feel it as soon as it negatively affects their property, rental profit, and their tenants. When it occurs, it is time to undertake some urgent measures. Here, I provide you with a step-by-step direction to handle such a situation. First, you need to solve the problem with communication between you and your property manager. In 80% of the cases, this is the cause of the problem. The property manager must inform you what's going on in the management of your property, concerning accounting, money transfer, rent collection and delays, maintenance works and repairs, renting vacant units, lease interruption, and tenant eviction. All that information must be transparent and available for you. Don't forget, it is your property. Stipulate in the contract what the manager must tell you and when. Normally, the reputable property management companies are eager to disclose fully.

If attempts to improve interaction with the property manager do not help, and you are still not satisfied with his services, then you should break the contract. You need to know in which cases you can terminate it without harming yourself. Like many other agreements, it provides for a penalty in the event of early termination. Ensure you do not face legal consequences for breach of contract. Otherwise, you might be involved in a lawsuit. It is necessary to prepare for avoiding this, strange as it may sound, at the stage of the contract signing. You should specify in advance all possible issues according to which you have the right to terminate the contract with no painful outcomes for you, and set them in the termination clauses. This can be when the property manager fails to perform the following duties in your best interests: does not necessarily try to fill vacant apartments, and they remain uninhabited for a long time; financial records and documentation are poorly maintained; there are violations in the accounting; costs of repairs and contractual services are overestimated; weak rent collection; late transfers and bill payments;

violations of fair housing laws; bad communication with residents; no response on their requests; bad interaction with you; and many other unpleasant issues. On my site, www.MakeItBigBelowTheBorder.com, you will find the list of termination clauses you can insert in the draft of your agreement. However, the main reason for termination is when the manager has broken the terms of the current contract. Make sure you are not subject to fines while canceling the contract, due to the reasons stipulated in the termination clauses. Another point to pay attention to is the duration of the contract. Use this provision to your benefit. While many property management contracts are annual, you may begin by signing a temporary contract to ensure you receive proven value from your property manager before committing for the longer term. Some property managers may understand your point and offer a short-term contract to secure your business. Insist on signing an agreement for a six-month trial period with the intention of signing the regular contract later. Then, clearly specify the duration of your contract you want in the property management agreement.

Another pitfall you can face when canceling your relationship with a property manager is not sending him a written notice to terminate a contract. Do it thirty days in advance; this term provision must be previously stipulated in the contract. Send the notice by certified mail and request a return receipt, so you will have a record confirming it is sent and the property manager received it. You must inform your tenants in writing about the change of the property manager. Provide the tenants with the information about who will manage the property from this point forward and who will be responsible for holding their security deposits. Make sure you receive copies of all papers related to your property, including leases, statements of all income and expenses by years, records of security deposits, etc. These documents must be sent to you right away upon the contract termination. When you find something inacceptable in your property manager's performance or when he is in breach of contract, do not defer a problem—make a quick decision about firing him. The more you postpone, the worse it will be for you. You must be tough at hiring and easy-going at firing property managers.

Remember, you have a list of ten other property managers from the moment you created your team. Besides, since purchasing your first property, you have already met many people in your area and found out which real estate management companies are popular. Quickly find another manager and carefully select him. Ask all the necessary questions about his performance and experience as we talked before. Carefully study the new contract and include all needed amendments protecting your interests. In many real estate markets, there is intense competition among them. Therefore, it will not be difficult to find a new candidate.

Focusing on Finding Right Tenants

The key to renting your house and not having problems with tenants is their proper selection from the very beginning. It is crucial to find safe and stable tenants who will pay on time, are willing to stay for a long time, won't trouble other residents, and won't spoil your property. I am convinced that to achieve this result, it is necessary to work seriously on tenant selection. To be more precise, you will control your manager, so he will do this job properly, which includes the measures for the advertising and marketing of vacant units, accepting phone inquiries, showing vacant units, accepting rental applications, and application pre-screening.

Advertising and marketing

It is imperative to know the social profile of your tenants. Ask your manager which people he sees as your customers—families with children, students, or seniors? Find out what usually attracts people in your area—the availability of a good school, the opportunity to find a job, or a location? Work out, with your property manager, an idea of how to entice good tenants. What should the advertising slogan be? What are the distinct advantages of your property, and what possible benefits can customers get if they choose your home? Ask what advertising methods your manager has accepted. A fruitful and conscientious property management company puts this matter on a firm footing. They should have enough experience in promoting properties of all their clients. Along with listing your property on MLS, Craigslist, Zillow.com, and Trulia.com, the property manager may publicize your house through the local newspaper or flyer distribution. Ask him to announce your home through social media, like Facebook and Twitter. The manager should prepare advertising plans to be used for further rentals, and you need to approve it in advance. Also, the role of a manager in the leasing of vacant units should be negotiated as part of the manager's duties and responsibilities in the contract. He must use diligent efforts to lease the house at rental rates and conditions acceptable to you, as the owner.

Tenant due diligence. The responsible attitude of the property manager toward tenant selection should be stipulated in the contract. Sometimes property managers prefer to outsource this function. Often, it makes sense; you can get a professionally made, complete report about every prospect. In reality, the majority of potential tenants do not have a complicated history that requires thorough verification. Accept outsourcing service only if it is not expensive. Ask your manager to deal with each case. Another issue may arise when a property management company, which usually runs real estate in more prestigious neighborhoods, may place too high requirements on prospective tenants. Always inquire about the rules and criteria of their selection. If you agree, reflect them correctly in the contract. However, make sure they do not lodge unverified and random people in your property, which needs little work and effort, especially after you made major repairs to your property. You do not want poorly selected and careless tenants to ruin your house. Also, stay away from discrimination violations while selecting new tenants; it might cost you a lot of money. Normally, good property managers have sufficient experience with this issue and do not allow such cases to happen.

Ask your property manager to apply the following criteria for tenant selection: their gross monthly income must be approximately three times the monthly rent; applicants should possess a good credit history, with not less than a score of 600; applicants must have reliable references about rental payment and housekeeping from previous landlords; never rent to a claimant with an eviction on their record within the last ten years; avoid persons with criminal issues, a recent felony, or a bad financial history.

Evictions and Terminations of Tenancy. Make sure the agreement says your property manager handles eviction and termination of tenancy. Many do not stipulate this point in the contract. As a consequence, you may experience problems. How can you arrange an eviction if you are in another city? What else do you need a manager for, if not to solve such an important issue? Your property manager's responsibilities will include property inspection when tenants leave. Also, the manager should arrange house cleaning, including floors, carpets, rugs, kitchen cabinets and appliances, bathtub, showers and toilets, windows and doors.

How to Avoid Getting Sued

You cannot protect yourself 100% against all possible lawsuits, but you must do your utmost to minimize the risk. First, make sure that your manager does everything possible to keep the house in a healthy and habitable condition. State in the contract that all management activities should comply with state and local housing legislation. Second, use proper legal structures to acquire the property. We have talked about it in the previous chapter. Then, take out an umbrella insurance that protects you from significant claims and lawsuits. Also, ask your manager to keep everything under control and fix all slippery staircases and broken handrails. Avoid mold issues in your property. Remove asbestos and lead-based paints at the stage when you repair the property. Ask your property manager to apply the practice of getting repairs done quickly when something breaks in the house and the tenants complained. Insist that your manager doesn't sign leases with tenants with dangerous pets. Keep the security issues in your house under control—put in an alarm system and bars on windows and doors if the property is located in a crime area. Instruct your property manager in writing to avoid discriminative issues toward tenants.

Now you know how to properly organize all necessary work for renting your home. Here, I highlighted the key points of your interaction with the property manager. If you can coordinate their actions in a right way, you will be able to retain and develop this great business that can generate cash flow and has a tremendous potential for the growth of your investment. In fact, this is not so difficult, and I'm sure you will succeed. You just must act and not be afraid of possible difficulties that lie in your path! Also, you are perfectly informed; this book discloses all the possible challenges that real estate investors experience. Don't forget to use the information and free resources available on the book's website, www.MakeIt BigBelowTheBorder.com. You should also have an idea of your future opportunities so you keep investing. You will need to know how to exit a project with profit, collect all the money, and redirect your investments to buying other properties. We will talk about how to do this in the most efficient way in the next chapter.

Chapter 10

Do You Have an Exit Strategy?
It's Better to Have at Least One

"Don't start a company unless it's an obsession and something you love.If you have an exit strategy, it's not an obsession."
– Mark Cuban

I want to underline the importance of taking real actions. Just simply reading this book doesn't provide you with the desired result. I hope you have already bought a property and have finalised a bid for repairs. Not yet? Well, don't lose your time, start acting! I believe it is important you take real steps toward your first property, even before finishing this book.

Here, we will talk about the exit strategy, which is the final stage in the life cycle of your real estate transaction. At the time you hired your property manager, and rented all your units, you wondered what's next. You are developing a wonderful business; you have great and stable tenants; your solid property generates sustainable cash flow. Excellent! What is your next plan? You may keep your property forever and even leave it to your children. You can also sell it for a profit after a while and live on that money or reinvest in another property. It's possible as well, after putting in new tenants, to refinance your house in six months and purchase a new property with this money. There are many options. In this chapter, I will help you to choose the best one. However, before this, you need to know all possible factors that may affect your decision.

Exit Strategy. Why It's So Important

So, what does the exit strategy mean? It signifies the intelligent, pragmatic scenario to sell the property or to withdraw from the deal in another way, assuming an investor gains a substantial profit from it. The task facing each real estate investor is to choose the path that will bring the most benefit. It is also important to have several possible exit options in advance because, in case of problems, you stick to your investment strategy and choose the best exit tactics available at the moment. Most importantly, by having a deliberate exit strategy in advance, you can avoid making an impulsive decision. In life, there are always changes and new circumstances that require us to be flexible in our thoughts and actions. It would be bad to miss the wonderful chances that the investments in real estate provide and to have to get out of business under unfavourable conditions. However, by creating an exit strategy, you help yourself to visualise your goals and the opportunities opening in front of you.

To be more efficient, try to work out in advance how to monetize your efforts. You shouldn't forget about that. You are paid when selling or renting your property. It's true; you contribute a lot of effort and money initially—you invest, overcome difficulties at finding new deals, prepare your expert team, acquire an investment property, take a loan, renovate the property and, only after that, you get the long-expected profit. To help yourself with this issue, you need to articulate your goals and your proper exit strategy, and adhere strictly to them.

Know about all pros and cons for each exit option and be able to evaluate them properly. The first decision you must make is to either keep renting your property or to sell it in the foreseeable future. If you want to keep your building, I respect this decision. Real estate will bring you a stable monthly income. However, there are two points to which I want to draw your attention. First, try to keep only properties that have a potential for growth. They must be located in a good area with positive dynamics for the next 10 years. Selected properties should have a solid look and a good, spacious room layout to please future customers. Second, particularly in the beginning of your real estate investor career, I advise you not to get emotionally attached to your property but treat it as a unique tool helping you to create a fortune in the most efficient way. You should know when to get rid of any property you buy so you may consolidate money to purchase something big later. Try to resist the temptation to keep the best houses for yourself. The wise choice is to use the funds from selling these houses to reinvest in something more ambitious that brings much more profit, as well as to benefit from all those financial instruments that are only available when investing in real estate. You can build a great restaurant and live well off its income, as the McDonald's brothers did. However, you can develop a huge, national-scale business empire around this, much like Ray Kroc did. What do you think? The choice is yours.

If you want to create something big, then you need to know which exit strategy is right for you. And some great possibilities depend on the conditions of the real estate market in your city.

Exit Behavior on Hot and Slow Markets

For a start, I introduce you to a general concept of the exit strategy proposed in my book, then we will consider how to apply it in different real estate cycles. As soon as the repairs are finished, you will rent out your property. It might take two to three months to find decent and reliable tenants. Then, you will stabilise the property during the next six to nine months. After that, you will go to refinance in a small local bank. To find the one who can lend you the mortgage, call as many banks as you can. If you have a list of thirty local banks, call all thirty. Choose those banks that provide at least 80% of the new market value of your property. When you get refinancing, pay off a construction loan you may have taken from a hard money lender. Invest the remaining money in a new distressed property. Then repeat the cycle.

The first house will bring you a rental income, from which you will pay all expenses and a new mortgage. The remainder will be your net income. Accumulate certain reserves for the safe and thorough management of your property. On the fifth year of renting your property, sell it. Before selling, try to assess the situation on the real estate market. Look also at the growth dynamics of property prices in your neighbourhood during this period.

What to do in a hot market

In this case, keep under control the price increase in your area every year. Sell immediately after five years. You will have a good profit; reinvest it into the new property.

What to do in a slow market or in case of a recession

If you are in a slow market after five years, and it is hard to sell your property at a decent price, keep it and continue to get the rental cash flow until the market straightens up and regains its lost positions. When real estate markets downturn, unfortunately, many property owners go bankrupt, and the demand for rent increases. Therefore, you will not lose money if you keep renting your property. You will have a certain margin of safety; you will have a wonderful house and good tenants, and this is always a great asset!

Why I Recommend Selling Property in Five Years

Why sell your property in five years? Many investors think of keeping their properties forever. Why sell it if it is a nice house that generates a positive cash flow and grows in value each year? Right. As I said, it depends on the goals of a particular investor, and I respect any decision. However, keep in mind the renovations in your house are getting old. Kitchen cabinets with countertops, appliances, finishes, floors, carpets, bathtubs, toilets, vanity cabinets, fixtures, faucets, etc. are a subject of constant depreciation over time. I haven't even mentioned exterior works. Think of which repairs you might need after ten years or in fifteen years? Will your future tenants want to live in a building where the last renovation was made fifteen years before? You will make all necessary cosmetic updates along the way.

However, in time, you will need to spend more and more on current repairs. It's like a car that requires more repairs and new spare parts over time. I prefer to sell properties relatively new and in good condition. I can count on a higher price. In emerging real estate markets, the difference between newly renovated buildings and ones in need of serious repairs may vary significantly.

There is another important strategic argument. By selling your property in five years, you will get a solid equity in it and, as a consequence, a real potential to sell it with profit. Undoubtedly, your debt to the bank will considerably decrease in these five years. You can also expect the market price will increase during this period. The repairs you initially made remain new, and the building will be in excellent shape. After selling it, you get a sufficient down payment to buy another property and raise the value of this newly acquired house through extensive renovation again. After the refinancing of that new property, you also have money to buy one more house and eventually get two new properties. However, if you do not sell your property in five years, and leave everything as is, then you will only have this house. If you sell it and repeat the entire operation described in this book, then you can get two new properties.

You have an opportunity to accelerate your investment. The number of houses you will acquire can increase exponentially. You need not accumulate them to infinity. Here, you can apply a pattern the same as in the Monopoly game—sell a few *green* houses to buy one big *red* hotel or, maybe, one large apartment complex. But that is another story. In this strategy, only heaven is the limit.

Prepare Your Property for Sale

Now, here are a few tips on how to prepare your property for sale. Imagine that five years have passed. It's time to sell the house to move forward. Let's suppose the real estate market is in good condition. It has decent growth dynamics. You successfully rent all your units. So, you will prepare your property for sale. The first issue you need to decide is whether to sell the house with the tenants or without them.

Ask your real estate agent. He or she should know the market and advise on which option is better for you to sell faster and at a higher price. Asking for advice makes sense because the situation in each market may vary. If you sell your property without tenants, then you need to plan the sale for a year in advance and do not renew the lease to them. After tenants have gone, prepare the house for sale. You will need to repaint all the rooms and fix everything that is broken. You must remove all garbage and personal things left behind after the tenants move out. Throw everything out. Leave nothing. I even recommend you consider a home staging because it will help you a lot. Houses with home staging are sold faster than usual. It will help your potential buyers visualize the space in your home. Choose a good expert with experience in your area. Look at his portfolio. Determine whether you like his design style. A real professional will advise you to choose the cost-efficient option and not overload with furniture. Ask in which premises you need home staging—usually it is a kitchen, a dining room, a living room, and a master bedroom with a master bathroom. That's all.

Don't forget to take care of the property. Make sure the lawns are always cut. Arrange a house cleaning every two weeks. Take care of protecting the house because you will leave it without tenants. I strongly recommend installing a security alarm system and bars on windows and doors if your neighborhood is not safe. It is necessary to take these measures to avoid vandalism and theft. Resolve the issue with insurance because the current one covers your property when it is with tenants. So, ask your insurance broker for a vacant dwelling policy.

Since you are selling your property with no tenants, you are deprived of the rental cash flow. This way requires more concentration and action; you are under the pressure of high expenditures, like mortgage, insurance, property taxes, and utility bills. Even if you provide the cash reserves to cover these costs within three or four months, a delay in selling for half a year can lead to undesirable consequences. Therefore, you need to prepare everything in the most efficient way to sell your property soon.

If you sell your house with tenants, then you need an entirely different approach. Here, an uninterruptible cash flow is a significant advantage. You are not constrained by time, so you can safely sell your property for a long time. Just prepare everything in advance and inform your manager and tenants you want to sell the property.

In this case, your customer base will be much narrower. Regular buyers, who want to buy a house for themselves and who are statistically the overwhelming majority of your prospects, won't be interested in a property with tenants. They could be interested only if the price is low enough or if they have time to wait for the termination of tenant lease agreement. They might need your house because either they want to reside within reach of their close friends or relatives who might live nearby, or they want their children to go to a good school next to your home. Therefore, if you want to sell your property with tenants, your potential clients are turn-key investors, who want to buy real estate ready for rent. The downside is that they know making money in real estate is when buying, so they will aggressively negotiate the price. It might take more time to sell the property if you do not accept their terms. Here, the most important thing is your attitude. Set yourself appropriately for a long selling process.

Although there are still tenants in your house, you still can do the improvement work. Prepare the exterior of your property for sale. Take time to landscape. Mow the lawn on time. Clean in common areas. Your house should have a beautiful and neat appearance. If you have a brick house, clean the wall bricks with a pressure washer. Repaint your vinyl siding exterior walls, if any. Common areas, entrance, front yard, and backyard must be fresh and welcoming.

Some Useful Tips to Market Your House

To sell a house successfully, you need to use the most popular marketing techniques. Since you are investing from another city, I advise you to arrange marketing through your real estate agent. Your agent should promote your property through different resources, the most powerful of which is MLS.

If you sell your house with tenants, and you are not limited in time, then do not use aggressive marketing tactics. Let your real estate broker take care of the advertising of your house; just ask what means he/she will use for this.

If you sell the property with no tenants, then ask your agent to organize an open house for your property with a preliminary distribution of the event's flyers in your area. Believe me; it's one of the best ways to market your house. Another good idea is to hire a skilled photographer and make professional photos of your property. You can even order a video tour of the inside of your house. It costs a couple hundred dollars, but it is worth it. It makes a difference because it attracts the attention of people who seek houses through MLS. You can also advertise your house for sale online, using Facebook, Instagram, and Craigslist. Besides, I advise you to promote your property through flyer distribution, covering your neighborhood; about 70% or more of your potential buyers live there.

Buyer's Selection

There is another point to pay attention to. It is the prequalification of a potential buyer for your property. Be careful when choosing buyers, especially reviewing their ability to get a mortgage and pay a down payment. My advice is to require the bank approval and proof of funds from every buyer when selling. Don't accept any offer without these documents! Ask your agent to take care of it. Otherwise, you risk wasting a lot of time while a buyer's lender considers the file and finally refuse to provide a loan. The mortgage procedure might easily take two to three months and include a long wait for the bank loan officer, underwriter, and legal department to examine the file. Your property will be considered pending and will not be available to other potential buyers. Although this period is limited by the financial contingency clause in the offer, a buyer may ask for its prolongation, arguing the bank has not yet completed the loan proceedings. You don't need such a situation. Ask your buyer to provide a bank preliminary approval letter before submitting an offer. Bank approval also means the buyer has a good credit score. You need to also ask for his or her proof of funds just to be sure he/she has enough money for down payment. You may require an extract from the buyer's bank account for the last three months. Another way to control this situation is by requiring the buyer to use your mortgage broker. A buyer may choose a negligent and irresponsive specialist, who will consume a lot of time with no results. So, do not pay for such a bad choice; recommend to him the best professional you know. At least, you will be sure your mortgage broker will find the best solution for your buyer and will do everything right.

If you want to speed up the selling procedure, you may propose owner financing to a buyer. This is when you act as a bank and provide a loan to your potential buyer, who was denied a regular mortgage, but who can pay it and wants to live in your house. Here, the buyer pays you the mortgage payments at the interest rate higher than the regular one. After a certain stabilization period, about 6 to 9 months, during which the buyer's ability to pay the loan is confirmed, you can resell his obligation to the note-buyer with a small discount. You practically get a full payment for your house. The advantage of seller financing is you need not wait long for the bank approval of your buyer's mortgage. Hence, you can sell your property faster and get the full asking price. Here, it is crucial to make proper due diligence of your buyer. Select no buyer with a low credit score. Otherwise, it will be difficult to resell notes. He should preferably have a *borderline* credit rating, barely enough to meet the high requirements of a conventional loan. Besides, he must have a stable source of income to pay you monthly payments on the loan. This is a reasonable requirement because, in case of problems with his monthly payments, you have to go through the formal foreclosure procedure.

There is another option to sell your property.

Lease Option as an Additional Method to Exit

Here, you are not selling your house; you are taking the commitment of selling it over a certain time. In return, you get the option fee upfront, which is not reimbursable. Besides, the buyer pays you the monthly lease payment, which is higher than normal rent. He or she undertakes to buy the house in a year or two. So, it is a lease with the option to buy your property at a fixed price after a certain time. If the buyer does not buy the house, or does not pay monthly lease payments, then all the payments made before, even the option fee deposit, remain with you. Sometimes it's painful for the buyer. The risk is that some of your clients may sue you, even though they have signed a lease-option contract. To avoid such a situation, check two important points with your attorney from the very beginning. First, ask whether the lease-option is allowed in your state and county. Second, inquire about what amount is desirable to put in as an option fee in your area, so the court can recognize it as a *valuable consideration* for initiating a lease-option contract, but not as a down-payment for a regular transaction. Usually, the option payment is not over five percent of the total transaction amount.

Lease-option is appealing to those prospects who do not have enough money for a full down payment or cannot take a mortgage now, and they need time to clean up their credit score. Some of your prospects have no possibility to buy now, but they are afraid that, in two years, the prices will be higher because the market is probably moving upwards in your area. So, they want to fixate them through a lease-option contract. Some people think they can move to another place in future, so they do not want to buy a house now. However, they still want to have an option to buy it in case their plans change, and they will stay in your house longer. As the seller, you also have benefits, because the buyer takes care of the property as his own. You get the lease payments, which are higher than normal rent. You are selling the house for the full asking price. You need not seek other buyers. Finally, you avoid paying a substantial cost at closing—the real estate agent's fee, which is 4–6% of the sale price. So, do not advertise your property through your agent in case of lease-option, because there is no interest for him/her. Take advantage of online resources and other marketing methods I mentioned earlier.

In this chapter, you got an idea how to exit from a real estate deal. This is where your journey in the world of real estate does not end. You must think about how to repeat this operation again, and how to make the next deal. You need to adjust the whole process, build a successful real estate investment system, and develop it further. Here, the most important thing is to grow. We will talk about that in the next chapter.

Chapter 11

Repeat and Grow!

"It always seems impossible until it's done."
– Nelson Mandela

You have made the first deal. You have refinanced or sold the property. Now, you are a real investor—a genuine real estate investment professional. You did it! You made a significant profit. You got experience. You know what to do next. You understand the specifics of this business. Sometimes not everything goes smoothly. Perhaps you faced some obstacles during the renovation, or it was difficult to refinance, but you stayed determined. Your next task is not to give up, but to be strong enough to go on. The only thing standing between you and your success in real estate is your doubt about whether to continue. Your intuition will tell you to go for another good deal, follow this proven strategy, and persist to achieve your goal. Below, I provide you with some tips to help you overcome your last hesitations.

Good News for You: The Next Deal Will Be Much Easier

Yes, the next deal will be much easier. The psychological factor will help here because you made a previous transaction. You should feel more confident, be ready to reinvest, and be hungry enough to start the process again. All members of your team are happy now: your real estate agent, your GC, your property manager. You have created a rapport between them and you. They are also ready for your next project. Besides, you need not seek other professionals for your second transaction. You have already tested your existing team. It will save you time. In general, all preparation works you made during your first operation will help you to perform the second one. Now, you just need to *Copy and Paste* it. So, then, the next deal. Copy and paste again. And so on.

Later, after making deals several times, you will be recognized by other people who have heard about your advance. Other people will know about your experience, knowledge, ability to do business, and your perseverance to bring it to the end. Some will want to be a part of your success and invest with you. As one great sage said, a journey of a thousand miles starts with a single step. So, repeat your first step. Make one more pace to meet your success.

More good news! 1031 Exchange

There is another helper for you. You may remember the funds received in refinancing are not taxed, since they are not formally an income. Also, there is the possibility to postpone the payment of capital gain taxes for a later period when selling your home in five years. What does this give you? When selling a house, you will save more money, the lack of which is especially felt on the first stages of investment in real estate. You need this saved money to reinvest in a new house. The more money you reinvest, the faster you grow your business.

This opportunity is provided by the US tax authorities in the 1031 Exchange rule stipulated in Section 1031 of the Internal Revenue Code. It allows you to postpone payments of federal and state taxes on gain capital. It's not a tax-free regime but a tax-deferred one. Payments of deferred taxes in the future will be not so substantial given your business will thrive and you have a lot of houses. There are limitations here. You must purchase the next property within 45 days after selling the previous one. It is an Identification period. Then, you should close this property during 180 days of an Exchange period. Sometimes, it's difficult to find good deals within this strict time frame, especially in the due diligence stage, when you may refuse potential houses. So, you may identify three properties at a time, in case some won't work out.

Another restriction stipulates you should exchange the previous house for a *like-kind* one. This term refers to the nature and use of the property, i.e., you may exchange a rental duplex for the same or another sort of commercial property, but not for a piece of land or a single-family house. Besides, the value of a new home must be the same or greater than that of a sold one. This works well when you decide in exchange to purchase larger rental buildings. However, it's possible to apply an Improvement exchange, where you can make improvements on your replacement property, and its value (including renovation cost, debt, and equity) is the same as or greater than the value of the exchanged house. The improvement exchange must also be completed within 180 days and for a *like-kind* property.

You cannot carry out the 1031 Exchange yourself. You are obliged to use services of a qualified facilitator, who holds your money after selling your house, while you seek for a new deal. At closing, a title company sends the balance after paying off all obligations on the property, including mortgage, to the escrow account of this qualified intermediator. If you cannot find a new property during the identification period, he or she will withdraw the entire amount of unpaid tax and will return the rest. Ask your attorney to refer a real professional to you. Usually, his services cost between $700 and $1000. Remember, deferring tax payments saves you considerably more money in the long-term than if you pay tax each time you sell the property. It permits your real estate business to expand faster.

Reinvest Your Money

One of the most important points in real estate is to save money. We have talked about how to save it by choosing the most favorable tax treatment. You must also retain the money you got as net profit. There are many enticements to spend it on your personal needs. You must be resistant to such temptations. The winner is not the one who spends today from the income received but the one who constantly invests saved money and efforts in the growth of his or her business. Reinvest again and again to create something big. Then you may spend money from that big wealth you have created. Be persistent and patient about that. Your business will gain momentum soon. Just stick to the system and be smart in spending your funds. There is also another reason that might keep you from reinvesting: it's a fear of losing money on the next deal. Do not succumb to negative thoughts. If the first transaction succeeded, then you will not lose money the second time.

Following my strategy, you have an excellent opportunity to reinvest in the purchase of new property immediately after refinancing the previous one. You just need to choose such a house so money from refinancing is enough for its down payment. I will give an example. Let's suppose you have purchased a distressed property for $110,000. The property needed renovation for $75,000. After repairs, its value increased to $285,000. Then, you rented it and, six months later, looked for refinancing. One small local bank offered you 80% of the current market value of your house, i.e., $228,000. You have already invested $185,000 as the total of the purchase price and repair cost. Even after reimbursing yourself this amount, you will get $43,000 as net cash. You should reinvest it. I even recommend you reinvest the total amount of refinanced money, $228,000.

Let's consider another point when you need to pay off a hard money loan. We assume you've borrowed $120,000, which is 65% of your initial costs.

65% * ($110,000 of purchase price + $75,000 of repairs) = $120,000 hard money loan

Pay off this hard money loan from refinanced money. It remains $108,000 for you ($228,000 of refinanced money - $120,000 of hard money loan). Reinvest this money. In this example, this amount is almost enough for you to cover the down payments of two houses. I mean, the same houses as your first one, the down payment of which was $65,000. (It's the difference between your total costs $185,000 spent on the property and the borrowed $120,000 hard money). After refinancing, $108,000 will remain in your hands. Add the missing amount from your money and buy two more houses. Here, things will go two times faster. Remember it's just invented figures, helping you to understand my investment formula. In real life, the numbers may vary.

Now, we consider an example of reinvestment after selling your home in five years. Here, there is one amazing point! After refinancing and reinvesting in two new homes, as in the first example, your first house is still there. It still belongs to you and brings you a monthly cash flow. This way, you can possess three houses in total.

What happens to your first house in five years? You will sell it. Suppose its market value rose from $285,000 to $325,000 this time. Your mortgage debt has declined from $228,000 to $208,000. After the repayment of the mortgage, $117,000 remains. Here, it is necessary to anticipate the real estate agent commission of about 5%, and other closing costs of 4%, which is, total, around $29,000. Eventually, there will be $88,000 in your hands.

$325,000 new market price in 5 years - $208,000 mortgage debt - $29,000 closing costs and agent fees = $88,000

Invest this money in the down payment of the next house. Then, refinance this next house and buy a second property for that refinanced money. In five years, you can sell the previous house and start projects for two new homes. Now, you understand the magic. You have a perfect system in your hands, working with no fail; so, don't hesitate to apply it now. Further, by illustrating figures of these examples, I want to show how you can make your first million in 5–6 years.

Making Your First Million in Equity in Five Years

I would like to continue the idea by using two previous examples. You invested $65,000 in the down payment of a house that requires repairs. The purchase price was $110,000 and repairs cost $75,000. You also took a hard money loan for $120,000. Then you paid off this loan after refinancing. You had $108,000 left. In the previous example, I suggested you add some of your money from outside and make down payments for two houses with $65,000 to each. Here, we apply a conservative approach and assume you invested in the down payment of only one house. You invested just $65,000 and you had $43,000 left. (You need this money to stabilize the transaction— suddenly, you may have some unforeseen expenses, or you might need to make a slightly higher down payment at $75,000. Keep them in reserve). Don't forget the previous house still brings you a stable rental income and is waiting for its turn to sell in 5 years.

The newly acquired house, you will do in the same scheme. You will make repairs and raise the property value. Then you will rent your property to the right tenants. It will be the culmination of the first year. It results in possession of two houses that bring a passive cash flow.

At the beginning of the second year, you will refinance the second house. It will remain about $108,000 in your hands again. You understand now what I'm talking about. You just need to repeat without stopping. Reinvest in your third house and increase its value through making repairs. Put in the tenants again. So, the second year will finish on this. The result is another house that brings rental profit. You will have three houses, in total.

You can even speed up the process because you have $43,000 left from the first home, and the same amount from the second house. Just invest them in the purchase of your fourth property. Here, it will be four houses, not three as the culmination of the second year.

So, you continue. The effect of the third year will be two new houses.

The outcome of the fourth year will be another two new houses. The result of the fifth year will be two new homes again.

The most important thing is not to stop; keep the momentum.

At the end of the sixth year, you will have about 12 houses. In those properties, which you bought in the first three years, the equity will be between $100,000 and $117,000 in each house. For the rest of the houses, it will be smaller but will increase over time. In this way, the total equity of all 12 houses will be over one million dollars. Besides, these 12 homes will bring you between $3,500 and $4,000 of net monthly rental income. It is about $45,000 in a year. Now, you will be an equity millionaire. If you look at the title of the book, you will see it is a guide of how to create a million in real estate. That's the way it is!

Yes, it is realistic. However, I did not say you will earn your first million quickly. This will take effort and time, five or six years, depending on the situation. Even if you have a forced delay or something goes wrong with the project, you can still earn it in seven or eight years. It will not be so important anymore. Unless you have made a bet with someone that you will earn this money in exactly six years.

Remember, for the fifth year, you will sell two of your first homes, which you bought at the very beginning. Each of these houses, while selling them, has the potential to purchase two more properties, as I mentioned earlier in this chapter. Every next year, you sell two houses and get four new ones, and so on, by increasing the number of your homes exponentially. When you collect a critical mass of twenty houses, you can sell some and reinvest in the purchase of multi-apartment complexes or new home construction. It is another topic for my next book, though.

All these examples with invented figures help visually illustrate the investment tactic plan. In real life, figures may differ, but the strategy and its algorithm remain unchanged.

Streamline Your System

After making the transaction two or three times, you will see this is not a complicated business. You can concentrate on working ON the business, instead of working IN it. You will quickly see the issues you can simplify in this system, making it easier for your execution. You also need to do this because the number of houses will increase every year, as I showed in the previous part; you must learn to manage many homes efficiently: seeking and selection of good deals; submission of offers; proper preparation of papers for construction, including the scope of work; work coordination of your general contractor and his crew; management of your property manager; selection of new members of your team. On our website, www.MakeItBigBelow TheBorder.com, you can have access to many documents and support materials that will help you in properly arranging your investment system. All these steps can be brought to automatic reflexes similarly to the operation on a conveyor belt. Perform it in the same way, so you do not need to fly to the city where you invest; you can do everything at a distance.

After the fifth transaction, think about finding yourself an assistant who will take over some of your responsibilities. First, he must perform as a project manager and take control over repairs. His or her second function is to control and coordinate the work of property managers in all your houses. You should choose a capable and knowledgeable local employee with experience in either construction or property management. Keep in mind that your role in this business is to perform as a visionary. You should control the accomplishment of the entire system and handle its expansion and growth through the skillful delegation of work to other members of your team.

When you have a proven system in place, everybody will notice it. It will also facilitate to attract investors into your business.

Bring Investors in Your Future Deal

It's possible to achieve a synergy in real estate growth by attracting *other people's money*. My strategy allows you to realize the entire potential laid out in this opportunity. Although there is a lot of controversy around whether to involve a partner in business, due to possible contradictions in the future, uneven distribution of functions, the need to share profits, incompatible goals and values of partners, I strongly recommend not to miss the opportunity to cooperate with people who wish to invest with you. Accept their help, their participation, and their money. Remember, you share with partners not only the profit but your risks, liabilities, expenses, and responsibilities. Be honest and respectful with them. Hold in high regard their interests before your own. Be disciplined in all commitments taken toward them. Act in a clear, organized, and energetic way. Remember, they will invest not in your strategy, not in your investment scheme, but in you. They will invest in your capacity to do business. So, demonstrate your high-level skills, knowledge, and leadership qualities as an investor.

Once you start the first deal, you can invite other investors who also want to put money in American real estate. Share everything in half, including expenses and responsibilities. It will reduce your risk remarkably. Earlier, in chapter 3, I told you where you can find a partner. The best way is to attend different real estate investment events and find like-minded people when networking. Another good option is to invite two partners, at once, and share your participation in three equal parts. Here, you reduce your financial risk ever more and can allocate responsibilities between partners, so the business develops faster.

There is another way to structure a deal with partners. It works when you have completed several transactions. By that time, you will have valuable connections in your target area. You will know the market and the people you may need for your business. So, you can search for a local partner for your next deals. Agree with him on equal participation—fifty-fifty. You will be responsible to invest the cash in down payment, and he will take care of a construction loan. It will be much easier to get financing if the primary partner is a local guy, who is also a US resident. To be eligible for a regular loan, he needs to have a good credit score. Later, after refinancing, you will return your invested money, and he will repay the construction loan. Besides, you feel more comfortable when there is another pair of eyes in place to monitor the progression of construction work and control a property manager.

The next option for shaping a partnership is after you hire an employee; your real estate business should be developed to be ready for such collaboration. When you have a well-working business, it's much easier to find private investors who will finance the entire deal, or part of it, with a down payment. If the investor finances the purchase price and repair costs, offer him 50% of the project. If he pays only the down payment, don't exceed 40%. Due to bigger responsibility, I recommend involving a local partner in the operation, who will take care of many functions of controlling the property in place. You can divide the remaining shares in half with him.

Eventually, your investor will receive the invested money after refinancing within one year. His share in the project will remain the same; he will receive 40% of the net rental income and 40% of the sale price in five years. It's a fantastic deal for him. He can also reinvest the same amount in your next project. It's like a revolving scheme. By circulating the same sum of money, your investor will get a significant portion in each newly acquired property every coming year! So, you and your investors are motivated to expand your business. I advise you to invite investors, especially when you increase the net rent income after creating an additional unit in the basement. Here, the cash flow looks attractive to both of you.

Focus On Your Investment Goals and Take Massive Actions

After reading this book, do two things to invest in real estate successfully. First, take massive actions and, second, create an entire focus on your investment goals and objectives.

Massive actions are important for any entrepreneur and investor so their first project does not fail from the very beginning. For that, it is paramount you will train your persistence and psychological endurance. First, decide whether you want to invest in real estate. If the answer is yes, then you must act immediately. Do not postpone; there will never be a better time than now to start investing. Your first actions are the preparatory stage of your project: searching for your real estate market and building your team. I hope my book will help you with this job. You can get a lot of useful information, as a free bonus, on the site www.MakeItBigBelowTheBorder.com. Do not skimp your time and energy on acquiring new knowledge and skills. Then, learn how to find a property with investment potential. Submit your first offer. Then the next one. Keep it up! Remember, after you decided to take actions, there is no more procrastination, or excuses. Instead, move rapidly and forcefully. Try to optimize your time without wasting it. While presenting offers, look for other real professionals in your team, network with other investors, and find out more information about your area. Do everything advisedly and without delay. If you do not like an expert, do not worry; thank him for the meeting and go look for another one. If you do no not love the property, look for the next one. Good deals always exist. It all depends on how much effort and patience you put in to find them. Be confident in yourself. You will succeed. Real estate is one of the most secure assets. It also has unlimited potential because many financial instruments allow attracting significant funds under it.

Do not fear problems. They exist in any business. No matter how excellent and flawless the strategy is, in real life, the most unexpected situations may arise. As for real estate, the problems will not be systemic. I have the courage to assume they can appear because of your improper attitude toward the project. You might not fully follow the proven methods. As a result, something will not work out. My strategy has a certain margin of safety. It assumes many professional people from your team are involved in the deal, and each knows his business well. They don't let your project fail. Providing legal support to your transaction in different contracts and substantial collateral provided by your property is also significant support for your project. Let's talk about focusing on your goals now. The full concentration on your investment objectives will not allow you to be distracted by any fears or doubts that will arise on your path. Try to get rid of all negative emotions. They harmfully affect your performance and can lead to procrastination and analytical paralysis. Do not let them dominate over you. Especially, do not succumb to questions like: What if...? Remember, by following this strategy, you are only taking a reasonable risk. So, work on your habits and thoughts. Try to be disciplined. At first, everything might go slowly. You might have to combine investment with your primary job. However, having developed the habit of doing it gradually each day, you can invest in real estate part time. Gaining experience and skills, you will reach a good speed, and you will become unstoppable in real estate. Be creative, listen to your intuition, and do everything with enthusiasm. Remember, your role is to be a visionary and a leader. This is your road to financial freedom, and to your prosperity. MAKE IT BIG BELOW THE BORDER!

About the Author

Nurlan Chulakov was born in Almaty, Kazakhstan. He graduated from Moscow University with a degree in Natural Sciences. Then he spent 10 years working for a French consulting group whose clients, the big western corporations, wanted to expand on new Kazakhstani infrastructure and hydrocarbon markets. At the age of 40, he moved to Canada and decided to change his career, devoting himself to real estate investments. He has experience investing in Canadian real estate; Montreal's daily newspaper, *The Gazette,* published an interview with him on April 27, 2013. Later, he decided to grow his portfolio by buying properties in US emerging markets. Today, he successfully invests in purchasing 2–4 unit properties in Chicago. Nurlan is pleased to assist others with the information and advice he has for investors throughout the world who are interested in purchasing the cash-flowing properties in the US. He is available to answer any questions about the subject at: nurlan@makeitbig belowtheborder.com

www.ingramcontent.com/pod-product-compliance
Lightning Source LLC
Chambersburg PA
CBHW060602200326
41521CB00007B/639